a handful of herbs

R Y L A N D

P E T E R S

& S M A L L

LONDON NEW YORK

Barbara Segall   Louise Pickford   Rose Hammick

a handful of herbs

inspiring ideas for gardening, cooking and decorating your home with herbs

with photography by Caroline Arber and William Lingwood

Senior designer **Ashley Western**

Senior editor **Henrietta Heald**

Location research manager **Kate Brunt**

Location research **Sarah Hepworth, Jenny Drane**

Production director **Meryl Silbert**

Art director **Gabriella Le Grazie**

Publishing director **Alison Starling**

Stylist **Rose Hammick**

Proofreader and indexer **Laura Hicks**

First published in the United Kingdom in 2001

by Ryland Peters & Small

Kirkman House

12–14 Whitfield Street

London W1T 2RP

www.rylandpeters.com

10 9 8 7 6 5 4 3 2 1

ISBN 1 84172 109 3

A CIP record for this book is available from
the British Library.

Printed and bound in China.

**Essential oils should not be used undiluted nor taken
internally except on medical advice. No responsibility
for any problem arising from their use is accepted by
the author or publisher.**

Contents

introduction

Every one of us feels that our own garden is a particular paradise, but the herb garden has the edge on them all. There is nothing quite like the rush of sensual pleasure that comes from simply brushing against a lavender bush, or stepping across a thyme or chamomile path.

These attractions don't end in the garden. Herbs can be brought into the house to be used fresh in cooking, or dried, frozen or otherwise preserved for later use. Some can be transformed into potpourri or used in different ways to perfume and decorate rooms, or to freshen drawers and clothes, while others fragrance baths or become simple, gentle cosmetics and lotions.

Gardeners of the past discovered, probably through trial and error, which plants were safe to use in food and for healing. Down the centuries herbs and other useful plants have come into our lives courtesy of various waves of invaders, travellers and soldiers. Herbs were first appreciated for their medicinal qualities. In Western history, the medicinal use of herbs dates from the first century AD, when the Greek physician Dioscorides set out the healing properties of more than 500 plants in what was one of the first descriptive herbals, his *De Materia Medica*.

In the herb gardens of today it is not uncommon to find the culinary, medicinal and folkloric traditions of the past combined with a modern appreciation of attractive plant forms. Most herb gardens are now enjoyed for the power-packed aromatic leaves of herbs such as rosemary, sage, thyme, lovage and chives, as well as for the simple but enchanting flowers and useful seeds that many herbs offer. It is this continuity of the past in our present homes that makes the bountiful summer harvest of these useful plants so evocative and especially satisfying.

If asked to define a herb, most people would say it is a plant used in cooking, but the true definition of the term is much wider. It includes trees, shrubs, biennials, annuals and herbaceous perennials that have culinary, aromatic, medicinal and cosmetic uses. In addition, many are excellent decorative garden plants. Some herbs are used for their foliage and flowers, others for their seeds or roots, and some for all four attributes.

Barbara Segall

LEFT **The deep pink blooms of an ornamental achillea bring a touch of flamboyance to a herb garden.**

super herbs

With an ancient record in folklore and medicinal history, basil is also a highly distinctive culinary herb, especially in Asian, French and Italian cuisines.

BASIL
Ocimum basilicum

Best used freshly picked, basil can also be frozen in leaf form or in made-up sauces. It combines well with tomatoes for a salad and is the main ingredient of pesto sauce for pasta. It adds piquancy to pizzas and to chicken and lamb dishes.

There are at least 13 different types of basil, varying in foliage, colour, shape, texture and aroma. Flavours range from aniseed to cinnamon and the sweet, spicy, clove-like scent of sweet basil. Basil can grow up to 45 cm (18 in).

O. basilicum 'Purpurascens' has purple leaves and pinkish flowers. *O. basilicum* 'Citriodorum' is lemon-scented with green leaves and white flowers. Anise-flavoured basil has pale pink flowers and a strong taste of aniseed. The tiny leaves of Greek basil, which grows in the shape of a small bush, offer the fullest flavour.

Plant basil in a herb garden or in containers in late summer, when there is no danger of frost or severely cold weather. In the herb garden grow it in a sheltered sunny site in light well-drained soil. If grown on in a container, basil should be kept well watered in dry conditions.

Basil has traditional uses as a digestive aid and a herbal tonic, as well as being used in aromatherapy.

Bay leaves were the foliage used in wreaths to garland winners and achievers in classical Greece and Rome.

BAY
Laurus nobilis

Glossy dark-green bay leaves are part of the bouquet garni, the traditional herb bundle used to add flavour to savoury dishes. Bay is also a good flavouring for sweet dishes, particularly rice puddings and other milk desserts; its delicate spiciness can be best enjoyed if the milk is simmered gently with the bay leaf before the other ingredients are added.

An evergreen tree with shiny aromatic, spicy leaves, small yellow flowers and black berries, bay can grow to 12 m (40 ft) but is generally slow-growing, and in containers its height is controlled. It can be clipped into geometric shapes or grown as an elegant ornamental standard. Shaped bay trees in pots are also useful in herb gardens as focal points to mark the meeting of paths or to emphasize a change of height.

Buy young plants and plant them in spring or autumn in rich, well-drained soil. Although bay will tolerate light shade, it prefers full sun. Protect young plants and plants in containers from frost with straw bales, bubble wrap or hessian windbreaks. Cut back any frost-damaged stems in spring. Pick leaves as needed throughout the year.

L. nobilis 'Aurea' has golden leaves and makes an attractive colour contrast in the herb garden. *L. nobilis* 'Angustifolia', the willowleaf bay, is also attractive as a container plant and in the garden.

Infusions made from bay leaves have been used to stimulate appetite or as an aid to digestion.

CHAMOMILE
Chamaemelum nobile

This hardy evergreen perennial is distinguished by flowers that resemble daisies, finely cut foliage – and a perfume that takes your breath away. Chamomile is widely used in cosmetics, soothing skin creams and other medications. Its dried flowers can be steeped in hot water to make a relaxing tisane, but it has no culinary uses. The creeping, non-flowering variety of chamomile tolerates light traffic, making it suitable for covering a short length of path or the ground under a bench.

Grow chamomile in light well-drained soil in full sun. It can reach 20 cm (8 in) in height. Chamomile paths should be kept weed-free or the weeds will overwhelm the chamomile plants, eventually destroying the fragrant pathway.

Non-flowering lawn chamomile, *C. nobile* 'Treneague', which has fernlike leaves, is used to create scented lawns and paths. Upright chamomile, which has daisy-like blooms, is grown in the border for its flowers, which can be used fresh or dried. The double-flowered form, *C. nobile* 'Flore Pleno', is an attractive addition to the garden, and its flowers are used to make chamomile tea.

The flowers, single or double, of upright chamomile have medicinal and cosmetic uses in facial steam baths and hair rinses; they also bring a soothing and relaxing fragrance to a bath. Dried flowers and leaves of chamomile can be added to potpourri.

A pineapple-like scent floats in the air when the leaves are crushed underfoot or gently squeezed between the fingers.

CHERVIL
Anthriscus cerefolium

A refreshing salad herb, chervil is also useful as a feathery and flavoursome garnish. Its light taste combines well with eggs, poultry and soft cheese. Although best used fresh, the leaves can be preserved by being frozen in ice-cube containers.

Chervil is highly prized in France, where it is often used in omelettes and as a component of the traditional *fines herbes* mixture.

Chervil is a hardy annual with pretty fernlike leaves and small delicate white flowers in late summer. It grows to 30 cm (12 in), thriving in a shady site in light well-drained soil. If planted as an inter-row crop, chervil takes advantage of shade from other row-crop plants. It dislikes root disturbance, so sow it direct into the growing site. Water plants well or they will bolt, flowering and setting seed too quickly, and you will lose flavoursome foliage. Pick the leaves through the summer.

Chervil plants can be grown indoors on a shady north-facing windowsill, but indoor plants will lack the vigour and flavour of plants grown outdoors. You can also sow seed in late summer for a winter crop, which will need some protection through the winter.

Rich in vitamins, chervil has traditionally been used as a treatment for digestive and circulatory disorders.

Chives (opposite page, left) bring a hint of onion to garnishes and salads, while
coriander (opposite page, right) adds piquancy to curries and other hot dishes.

CHIVES and GARLIC CHIVES
Allium schoenoprasum and *A. tuberosum*

Chives have spiky green leaves and mauve flowers, while garlic
chives, or Chinese chives, have garlic flavour in their strappy
leaves and white starry flowers that appear in late summer.
The chopped leaves of both types combine well with egg dishes
and are useful for garnishes and in salads. Chives are also
among the ingredients of the *fines herbes* mixture.

With their attractive flowers and good foliage, chives fit well into the
flower garden. They make an informal edging for part of a kitchen
garden and, if planted into spaces in paving, will eventually spread
to make their own shapely patterns in the paving gaps.

The spiky leaves shoot from the underground mini-bulbs in spring.
They grow to about 25 cm (10 in) but can be harvested once they are
about 10 cm (4 in) above ground. Either pull leaves from the clump or
cut off a handful with a pair of sharp scissors.

In late spring even spikier shoots carrying the flower buds start to
appear. Chive flowers come in a range of pinky-mauve tones, as well
as in a new form that is green to white. The flower heads, made up
of numerous tiny flowers, are also edible and look attractive in salads.
They are at their juicy best just as the buds begin to open.

Chives grow well in containers but will need extra attention to
prevent them from drying out. Young plants can be kept on a
windowsill or planted out in the sunniest site in the garden.

Chives have a traditional medicinal use as an antibiotic and as an
appetite stimulant and a digestive aid.

CORIANDER
Coriandrum sativum

A strongly aromatic, short-lived annual, coriander is grown for
its seeds and for its deeply cut, parsley-like leaves that bring
spice and flavour to desserts and savoury dishes alike. It bears
a profusion of tiny white flowers. For the full effect of their
flavour to be appreciated, coriander leaves should be added
towards the end of the cooking time.

The dainty pinkish-white flowers that appear from early summer
are followed by bead-like seeds, which are used in baking cakes
and biscuits as well as in curries, chutneys and pickles. The leaves
are added to stews and salads or used as a garnish. Plants grow to
a height of about 60 cm (24 in).

C. s. 'Morocco' is a good form for seed production, while *C. s.*
'Cilantro' produces abundant well-flavoured foliage. There are forms
of coriander that are offered for seed production as well as those
for leaf production.

Coriander grows well in a sunny spot in light well-drained soil.
It needs a long hot summer for best seed production. Sow seeds
in spring into the growing site and cover them with a cloche until
established. Young plants should be kept well-watered and free
of weeds until they are established. Pick young leaves before the
mature ferny leaves develop.

Seeds tend to fall before they can be harvested, so the flower heads
need to be picked before the seeds are fully ripe. Cover the flower
heads and store them in a warm, dry, airy place so that the seeds
can ripen. Store the seeds in an airtight jar.

A cleansing spiciness is dill's gift to fish, soups and salads.

DILL
Anethum graveolens

An excellent partner for fish in any form, hot or cold, dill is particularly renowned as an ingredient of the Scandinavian marinated-salmon dish gravadlax. Its fresh young leaves bring spice to salads, egg dishes and soups. The seeds, together with the flower heads, are used in pickles, preserves and chutneys. They are tasty with rice and cabbage, or as a flavouring for savoury bread, and are also used ground in curries.

A hardy annual with aromatic feathery leaves and clusters of yellow flowers in midsummer, dill grows to between 60 cm (2 ft) and 150 cm (5 ft), depending on variety. The seed needs well-drained soil, full sun and a sheltered site. Sow in the herb garden in spring, once the soil has warmed up. Since dill grows tall, it is not ideal in containers, but they can be useful for a first sowing.

Water seedlings and thin out to 20 cm (8 in). If necessary, support plants with a light framework of hazel twigs. Water regularly in dry seasons, or the plants will bolt and flower, and leaf harvest will be minimal. Pick leaves as needed when they are fresh and young.

Harvest seeds for culinary use before they ripen completely on the plant. Cut the flower heads off the plant, put them in paper bags and leave them to ripen in a warm dry place. When the seeds are dried, clean off the husks and store the seeds in airtight jars, ready for use.

Many seed companies differentiate between leaf and seed dill. *A. g.* 'Sari' is a variety grown for high yields of leaves with short stems. *A. g.* 'Herkules' is highly aromatic, while *A. g.* 'Dukat' is selected for its good leaf production. (All these varieties also produce good seeds.)

Dill is used as a calming treatment for upset stomachs and to alleviate insomnia. Ground seeds are sometimes used as a substitute for salt.

Fennel's wispy foliage is one of the delights of the herb garden in spring.

FENNEL
Foeniculum vulgare

This herb's bright-green leaf shoots unfurl in spring from pale leaf sheaths in which they are tightly packed like small parcels, scented with an unmistakable aroma. Fennel is distinct from Florence fennel, which is grown as a vegetable. The leaves are a flavoursome addition to salads and soups and make a good garnish. Bronze and green fennel can be combined to make a topping for salads. Both types are good partners for fish dishes. The seeds are also used in cooking and to make teas or tisanes. The flower heads can be used in pickling, and the leaves for flavouring oils and vinegars.

Fennel is a hardy perennial grown for its finely cut aromatic leaves in spring and summer and umbels of small yellow flowers in summer. It can grow to more than 2 m (6½ ft) and self-seeds – so be ruthless when you see fennel seedlings in spring. The ornamental quality of its foliage makes bronze fennel, *F. v.* 'Purpureum', rewarding to grow. It has chocolate-brown feathery leaves, which contrast well with the green of ordinary fennel. The aroma is the same.

Grow fennel in a sunny site in rich well-drained soil. Sow into the growing site in late spring, or in containers in a greenhouse for earlier germination. Either thin or transplant, leaving a space of 50 cm (20 in) between plants.

Pick fennel leaves as needed through the spring and summer. The seeds should be harvested in autumn when they are ripe. Divide established plants of common fennel in spring or autumn. Try to segregate plantings of dill and fennel, or they will cross-pollinate.

Fennel has traditionally been used as a treatment for a wide range of conditions, but it is now most closely associated with the prevention of obesity.

Individual cloves of garlic can be used whole or chopped, crushed, or roasted in their skins to flavour savoury dishes, salads, salad dressings and bread.

GARLIC
Allium sativum

Several separate small cloves wrapped in a paper-thin skin that ranges in colour from rose-mauve to white are the components of a garlic bulb. Bulbs bought fresh from French markets or home-grown have an unbeatable flavour. Garlic is the main ingredient of many typical Mediterranean sauces, such as aioli, and is also valued for its health-giving effects.

Garlic has leek- or onion-like foliage and grows to 30 cm (12 in). It does best if grown in fertile well-drained soil in a sunny position. Plant individual cloves in spring, in rows 30 cm (12 in) apart, and keep them well watered, especially in dry periods.

Lift bulbs in summer and leave them on racks or in wooden boxes to dry off for a day or two in good weather; then hang them up in bunches in a dry, airy shed.

There are several different varieties of garlic available, with varying strengths of flavour; bulb and clove sizes also vary. *A. sativum* has white flowers, while *A. scorodoprasum* (also called rocambole) has a mild-flavoured bulb as well as edible bulbils mixed with flowers on its flower heads. Elephant garlic, *A. ampeloprasum* – which has a huge single onion-like bulb – is often available at supermarkets. Buy several bulbs, some to use and some to plant for next year's crop.

Traditionally used in the treatment of many conditions, garlic has been shown to lower blood pressure slightly and to boost the body's immunity to infections; it also has antiseptic qualities.

Long valued for its cleansing properties, and associated with fresh-smelling linen, lavender takes its name from the Latin for 'to wash'.

LAVENDER
Lavandula species

Lavender flowers can be used in baking and jam-making or to flavour sugar. More often, the dried flowers and foliage are used to perfume rooms or packed into muslin sachets and hung up in wardrobes. Flowers destined for potpourri or for making up into lavender bottles or bunches should be harvested as soon as they open, when the colour and aroma are at their most intense.

With grey-green, softly textured, highly aromatic leaves and (depending on species and variety) deep-blue, purple, white or pink flowers, this evergreen shrub grows up to 1 m (40 in). It thrives in a sunny, open site in well-drained, slightly sandy soil. *L. angustifolia* 'Hidcote', which has a uniform, compact shape and produces very deep-blue flowers, is a good choice for edging a path or small border. There are also forms with green, white or red flowers. Some lavenders, including *L. stoechas* and woolly lavender, *L. lanata*, are less hardy and need winter protection.

Lavender is useful as an edging or a hedging plant for a path or small parterre. Provided that you use plants of the same species or variety, the uniformity of shape and colour make it useful in formal as well as informal situations. It tolerates clipping into a variety of shapes. Cut back any woody stems in autumn and remove spent flower heads left on the plant from the previous season's flowering. Sow fresh seed in late summer or autumn. Transplant seedlings to 60 cm (24 in) apart or 30 cm (12 in) if growing as a hedge. Take cuttings in summer.

Lavender has been used therapeutically for its calming effects, as well as in the production of cosmetics and perfumes.

LEMON BALM
Melissa officinalis

A powerful lemon scent, released when its leaves are brushed against, and a fresh zesty flavour help to tip the balance in favour of lemon balm, which can become invasive in a small garden. It grows in soft mounded shapes that suit the front of a border. Leaves of lemon balm give a strong citrus flavour to salads.

Lemon balm is a hardy perennial, growing to 1 m (40 in) when in flower. Its rather insignificant flowers are carried on untidy-looking stems from midsummer to autumn. Lemon balm can be useful for areas in shade, as long as it is planted in well-drained but moist soil.

M. officinalis has plain green leaves. *M. o.* 'Aurea' is a golden-and-green variegated form that is very useful for introducing bold splashes of colour to the herb garden. *M. o.* 'All Gold' has yellow foliage.

The variegated form of lemon balm in particular combines well with other plants, but its flower stems should be snipped off to encourage leaf production. Once the flowers have formed, the yellow variegation tends to deteriorate.

Cut back flowering stems in late autumn to contain the tendency to self-seed. Pick leaves when required for fresh use and to dry or freeze. Sow seed in spring and divide established plants in autumn or spring.

A few leaves of fresh lemon balm in boiled water make a tasty tea, which has traditionally been used to relieve the symptoms of stress and tension.

To make the most effective herbal tea, harvest lemon balm before it comes into flower, when the essential oils are at their strongest.

Often reaching 2 m (6½ ft), lovage has a height and stature that make it useful as a tall accent plant at the centre of a kitchen herb garden.

LOVAGE
Levisticum officinale

Lovage has a strong spicy flavour and a long history in traditional English cookery. Its foliage slightly resembles that of celery.

A hardy perennial with large dark-green leaves, lovage can grow up to a height of 2 m (6½ ft). Clusters of small pale-ochre flowers, resembling those of parsley, appear in late summer. It does best in a sunny site in rich well-drained soil. Plants should be watered regularly until established.

Lovage looks attractive near angelica, and if grown at the base of a rose will hide the rose's bare stems. Divide plants in spring or autumn every two or three years. Pick leaves when they are needed and seeds when they are ripe.

Lovage adds spiciness to food. Fresh leaves and stalks can be sprinkled into soups and stews for a meaty flavour, or blanched and eaten as a vegetable. Young leaves are delicious in salads and make an elegant garnish for savoury dishes. Seeds are sometimes added to biscuits before baking. They can be crushed and used as an ingredient of mixed-herb marinades, and are valued as a remedy for digestive complaints.

Every herb garden should have at least one type of mint. With aromas and flavours for all occasions, mints also have much to offer in the shape of ornamental leaves and flowers.

MINT
Mentha species

Chop mint into vinegar and mix it with sugar and a little warm water to make mint sauce, the natural accompaniment for roast lamb. Mint jelly, made with apples and mint, is also satisfying with lamb dishes. In Middle Eastern countries mint is used in cooked and cold food, as well as in drinks such as mint tea.

The genus *Mentha* includes some 25 species of perennials grown for their leaves, which are usually oval to lance-shaped and toothed at the edges. The ornamental flowers, ranging from deep mauve to light pinky-lavender in colour, attract bees and butterflies.

Mint thrives in full sun in well-drained but moist soil. Set young plants out in spring or autumn, and divide clumps that are growing in the ground in autumn. Mint will grow equally well in light shade and, as long as there is a source of water, provides good ground cover. To restrict its rapid sprawling growth, plant mint in a deep plastic or tin container, and sink the container into the ground.

Gingermint (*Mentha* x *gracilis* 'Variegata') has a spicy flavour and green leaves splashed with yellow. Pineapple mint (*M. suaveolens* 'Variegata') has woolly-textured green leaves, marked irregularly with creamy white, usually at the margins. Spearmint (*M. spicata*) and peppermint (*M.* x *piperita*) – both vigorous, spreading plants with attractive flowers – have the flavour traditionally associated with mint. Probably the most highly scented variety is lemon or eau-de-Cologne mint (*M.* x *piperita* 'Citrata'), which has a bronze tone to its leaves and stems. The perfume of its leaves is overwhelming if it is eaten, so it is better enjoyed as an aromatic foliage plant.

Mint is at its most aromatic before it comes into flower, so cut it back to encourage leaf production. Harvest the leaves through the growing season – they can be used fresh or dried, or frozen for later use. Mint may succumb to mint rust, which shows as rusty markings on the leaves. Remove affected plants and burn them, sterilize the soil, and replant with new healthy plants in another part of the garden.

OREGANO or MARJORAM
Origanum species

Oregano and wild marjoram are two names for *Origanum vulgare*, whose spicy aromatic leaves add zest to many meat and tomato dishes, and are an indispensable ingredient in Greek and Italian cuisines. The herb's various types of foliage and flowers also provide subtle ornament in the herb garden.

There are many other species of marjoram belonging to the *Origanum* genus, the more decorative of which can be used as edging plants or in mixed borders, where their attractive flower stems and aromatic leaves can be readily enjoyed. Some marjorams, including sweet marjoram (*O. majorana*), are half-hardy or tender – either grow them as annuals or protect them in winter.

Golden marjoram (*O. v.* 'Aureum') and gold-tipped marjoram (*O. v.* 'Gold Tip') provide wonderful splashes of colour in a herb garden. Golden marjoram has clusters of pretty tubular flowers in summer. Its foliage is a lemony-golden colour and makes a good display in the herb garden – but it should be planted in a semi-shady site to avoid leaf scorch from the sun. Gold-tipped marjoram has green leaves tipped with gold, and needs to be grown in a site that is not too shady or it will lose the variegation.

Compact marjoram (*O. v.* 'Compactum') grows to 15 cm (6 in), with a spread of 30 cm (12 in), and makes a good ground-covering mat of foliage. Pot marjoram grows up to 45 cm (18 in) and is propagated from cuttings.

Of the several different forms of oregano or marjoram that can be used in cooking, the best are Greek oregano (*O. v.* subsp. *hirtum*) and pot marjoram (*O. onites*). Some, including *O.* 'Kent Beauty' and *O. laevigatum* 'Herrenhausen', are generally regarded as decorative plants in the herb garden rather than for culinary use.

Oregano or marjoram does not need pruning as such, only the cutting back of flowering stems in late summer and of all stems to ground level in autumn.

For cooking, choose Greek oregano or pot marjoram. The former keeps its flavour when dried, but the latter is better used fresh.

Part of the traditional *bouquet garni*, parsley (opposite page, left) is also a popular garnish, while rosemary (opposite page, right) is a classic partner for lamb.

PARSLEY
Petroselinum crispum

A basic herb of many cuisines, parsley is one of the main components of the *bouquet garni* herb bundle. You can use the leaves chopped up or whole in salads, as a garnish or as a flavouring for sauces and soups.

There are several varieties of curly-leaved parsley, with tightly curled moss-like leaves. All grow as low compact plants during their first year and flower in their second year. Also attractive, but much larger, is flat-leaved parsley – *P. c.* 'Italian', or Italian or French parsley. It grows to a height of 30 cm (12 in). Its foliage is flat, and the stems and leaves are delicious either in salads or in cooked dishes.

Parsley is a hardy biennial that needs to be handled gently when it is transplanted because root disturbance will trigger its survival mechanism and set it in flowering mode too early. It prefers moisture-rich soil and partial shade. Buy plants in spring or autumn. Cover autumn-planted parsley with fleece or a cloche in winter to ensure a good supply of fresh herb.

The chopped leaves of parsley freeze well, and whole leaves can be dried for winter use. You can use parsley to make an alternative to Italian pesto sauce (usually made with basil), for parsley butter and in homemade cosmetics.

It is said that chewing parsley after drinking alcohol or eating garlic freshens the breath.

ROSEMARY
Rosmarinus officinalis

The delicate flowers and strongly aromatic leaves of rosemary are ornamental in the herb garden and have long been valued as ingredients in cooking, herbal cosmetics and traditional remedies. The leaves can be dried or frozen for later use.

Rosemary has spiky aromatic leaves on woody branches. It is a hardy evergreen perennial in most areas, but may need protection in harsh winters. Upright forms can reach 2 m (6½ ft) in height, and the prostrate form spreads and trails. Harvest from growing tips to keep the plant bushy and encourage foliage production. Rosemary flowers in summer, with, depending on species and variety, small aromatic blooms in pink, white or blue.

R. o. 'Prostratus' is a tender trailing or prostrate form with blue flowers. *R. o.* 'Albus' is hardy and has white flowers. For a tall rosemary hedge, choose *R. o.* 'Miss Jessopp's Upright'. 'Silver Spires' is a rediscovered old rosemary that was popular in Tudor times; it has silvery variegated leaves and is attractive in any season. 'Majorcan Pink' is half hardy and has pink flowers, while *R. o. lavandulaceus* is tender with blue flowers. *R. o.* 'Sudbury Blue' has delicate deep-blue flowers.

This herb prefers a sunny site with a little protection from cold winter winds. Good drainage is essential. Remove any stems that die back in cold weather and cut back the plant to keep it in shape after flowering. Take cuttings in summer. Pick leaves when needed, but remember that the aromatic flavours are at their best before flowering. Whole stems or sprigs can be dried or frozen for later use. For drying in bulk, harvest in late summer.

Use rosemary flowers and chopped young leaves in salads. Sprigs of rosemary can be laid on joints of meat before roasting; the leaves are added to herb butters, jams, jellies and summer drinks, and are used to flavour sugar for desserts. Rosemary salt is good for seasoning meats and marinades. The herb is an ingredient of some homemade and proprietary skin cleansers and hair conditioners.

SAGE
Salvia officinalis

Sage has been grown as a medicinal and culinary plant since ancient times. The name Salvia comes from the Latin word *salvere*, meaning to heal or save, and common sage – known for its astringent qualities – has been widely used as an antiseptic and cleansing herb in remedies and cosmetic preparations. Gargling with an infusion of sage can help to relieve the pain of a sore throat.

A hardy evergreen shrub with aromatic and decorative leaves, sage is as versatile in the kitchen as it is ornamental in the flower garden. It is used in numerous meat dishes, sometimes mixed with onion, and in salads, as well as in flavouring salt, oil and vinegar.

There are many sages that look decorative in the border, including *S. o.* 'Tricolor' with leaves variegated in purple, pink and white. Common sage has greyish-green leaves. Purple or red sage (*S. o.* 'Purpurascens') has purple-grey leaves, while golden sage (*S. o.* 'Icterina') has golden-green leaves.

Sages like full sun, an open site and light, well-drained soil. Replace plants that become too woody. Take cuttings in spring or mid-autumn, or layer branches *in situ*. Common sage and its varieties can be grown from seed, sown direct into the growing site when danger of frost is past, or in seed trays, cells or plugs, where temperatures of 15–21°C will ensure germination after two or three weeks.

If you are growing sage primarily for its useful leaves, cut out the flowering stems; pick leaves whenever you need them for cooking.

The classic herb for pork dishes, sage is often combined with apple sauce to form one of the best-known partnerships in English cuisine.

SORREL and BUCKLER LEAF SORREL
Rumex acetosa and *Rumex scutatus*

Sharp and clean to the taste, sorrel is an often undervalued element of the herb garden. Made into a sauce, it is a refreshing accompaniment to oily fish and adds piquancy to casseroles and stews. Buckler leaf sorrel (pictured), which has a milder taste, is particularly good in salads or as an alternative to spinach.

One of the traditional herbs of French cuisine, sorrel is a herbaceous perennial that, once established, will be in the herb garden for ever. It dies down in winter, but in spring its fresh green leaves appear – and at that time are at their tangy best for use in salads or sauces.

There are two sorrels that are useful in the kitchen and the garden. Common sorrel or garden sorrel (*R. acetosa*) is a strong-growing herb that makes large clumps of shield-shaped leaves, which should be eaten before the plant flowers; tall stems shoot up from the leaf mounds in summer, and the leaves on these stems do not taste as good. Small, unremarkable blooms are carried at the ends of the branched flower stems.

Of greater attraction in the garden is buckler leaf sorrel or French sorrel (*R. scutatus*). This comes in a green form and a more interesting silver-variegated form, 'Silver Shield', which has a marbled silvery centre to the leaf and gives good ground cover.

Sorrel is valued mainly for its culinary attributes, and has been used to treat blood disorders, but it has a high oxalic acid content and, if consumed in large quantities, may be harmful, especially to the kidneys – so use with caution.

Sorrel is one of the unsung treasures of the herb garden, especially when included in a sauce to serve with oily fish. Its tangy leaves can also be chewed to relieve thirst.

Tarragon packs a powerful punch in its narrow lance-like leaves. Often teamed with chicken, it is also the herb used to make sauce Béarnaise.

TARRAGON
Artemisia dracunculus

The fiery aniseed flavour of tarragon makes it perfect for spicing meat and fish dishes. The leaves also add piquancy to oils and vinegars and are excellent in marinades. Pick the leaves during spring and summer to use fresh, and in late summer to freeze for winter use.

French tarragon is a half-hardy perennial with narrow, pale, greenish-grey leaves. It can grow to a height of 1.5 m (5 ft) and in summer produces insignificant flowers which never reach maturity. This means that tarragon does not produce viable seed so can be propagated only by using root or stem cuttings.

Grow tarragon in light well-drained soil in a sunny site, and cut it back in autumn. Protect the crown with a covering of conifer foliage or straw during winter. Divide plants in spring or autumn.

There is a less tasty but more vigorous form of the herb called Russian tarragon (*A. dracunculoides*), which is often sold wrongly labelled as French tarragon. This species is very hardy and will survive winters without protection, but it is worth growing French tarragon for its flavour, which is far superior to that of the Russian variety.

Although it has no modern medicinal uses, tarragon was once valued as an antidote to snake bites.

THYME
Thymus vulgaris

An evergreen that can be used freshly picked all through the year, thyme is a component of *bouquet garni*. Both the flowers and the leaves are good in salads and are used to flavour oils, vinegars and marinades, as well as stocks and stews. Thyme is commonly added to stuffing for chickens. It combines particularly well with rosemary.

Thyme is a hardy evergreen sub-shrub with small, powerfully aromatic, spike-shaped or round leaves. There are variegated silver and golden forms.

The most vigorous and most useful for basic flavouring is common thyme (*T. vulgaris*), which has deep-green leaves and is a many-branched woody sub-shrub. It has mauve flowers. *T. v.* 'Silver Posie' has silver variegated leaves and a good flavour. *T.* x *citriodorus* is a shrubby thyme, with small green lemon-scented leaves and pink flowers.

T. x *citriodorus* 'Silver Queen' is variegated with creamy silvery leaves, rosy-pink buds and a strong lemon scent to its leaves. *T. serpyllum* 'Snowdrift' is a creeping thyme that carpets the ground in white when in flower.

The herb is versatile enough to be grown in the garden, on rockeries or in containers. The low-growing forms can be used to make attractive flowering paths or fragrant mats at the feet of benches. On a patio, plant up cracks in or gaps between paving to make aromatic stepping stones.

Grow thyme in full sun in well-drained soil. After flowering, cut back the plant to promote new growth and bushy shapes. Replace plants every few years, when they become too woody and open at their centres.

Thyme has a traditionally been used as an antiseptic.

Both upright and creeping forms of thyme produce aromatic leaves and attractive clusters of small pink, mauve or white flowers, which are as useful as the foliage in flavouring food.

gardening with herbs

how to grow herbs

Herbs are versatile plants that grow well in most types of garden soil and in most conditions. Their numbers can be increased by dividing plants or taking cuttings. Seed can often be sown direct into the ground – or you can sow it in pots and grow the new plants in windowsill propagation units or in a greenhouse.

Sow seed of hardy annuals direct into the soil in spring either in a seedbed or in their growing sites. Half-hardy herbs can also be sown in their growing sites once all danger of frost is past. Sow the seed in rows and just cover it with soil; water in well and thin out when seedlings are well established.

Sowing indoors produces plants ready for planting out as soon as the soil warms up and the seedlings have been hardened off in spring. Almost fill seed trays or cellular modules with soil, firm the surface down and water the compost or stand the trays in water. Leave the trays to drain before sowing fine seed into the compost surface. Space out large seeds and sieve a thin covering of compost over

LEFT **Use sharp clean scissors to harvest herb flowers such as those of lavender. Cut low down on the stem, so that you have long stems to tie into bundles for drying. Harvest on dry days, when the sun has just burnt off the dew and before it gets too hot. Lay the harvested material into a trug or basket and keep it in the shade until you are ready to use it. Harvest only the amount that you can work with in a short time, or the flowers may begin to deteriorate and wilt.**

SEQUENCE STARTING FROM FAR LEFT **Put a label in place before you sow. Empty the seed packet into your hand and then take a pinch of seed, or one seed if they are large, and place it in the trench or hole. Just cover the soil and firm it down with the back of your hand. Mark the line of the row with a trail of coloured gravel, especially if sowing parsley, which is notoriously slow to germinate.**

them. Put the trays in a heated propagator, with an even temperature of 15°C (59°F). Once the seeds have germinated and are large enough to handle, transplant them into small individual pots. Harden off by leaving them outside during the day and returning them to the greenhouse at night, until they are acclimatized to outdoor conditions.

Before buying a herb that is ready to plant out in the garden or to grow indoors, check that it has no obvious disease or pest problems; avoid plants that are root-bound or have damaged stems. Plant out your new herb as soon as possible, but not during the hottest part of the day. Dig a hole large enough to take the rootball, and remove any weeds from the soil. Put the plant in the hole, backfill with soil, then firm the surface of the soil and water the plant well. In dry conditions water the plant daily until it is well established.

Evergreen herbs such as bay, rosemary, sage and thyme can be harvested from outdoor and indoor herb collections all year round, as can herbs that you have forced into growth in winter, such as mint, tarragon and chives. Annual herbs, including basil, perilla, rocket, dill,

nasturtium and coriander, are at their best in spring and summer – late summer in the case of basil. Since herbaceous perennial herbs including fennel, lovage and comfrey die back in winter, their harvest period is during the spring and summer.

When each plant has produced good leafy growth, harvest it in an even way, to maintain a well-defined shape. For a handful of leaves to add to salads or cooked dishes, pick the herbs just before you want them, at any time of day.

To promote the vigorous growth of your herbs or to increase their numbers, divide the plants in early spring when they are still dormant, or in autumn when the growing season is coming to an end. In autumn, before dividing, cut back all the spent flowering stems. Then use a fork to lever the clump out of the ground. When it is loosened, lift it out and place it on the soil surface.

The traditional way to divide large plants is to place two forks back to back in the centre of the clump and prise the two sections of the plant apart. Keep on doing this to each section until you have reduced the size of the original clump and produced several new sections ready for replanting. Herbs such as chives can be prised apart by hand. Most perennials, such as marjoram, chives, echinacea, tarragon, sorrel, creeping thyme and lovage, grow to form large basal clumps. The growth at the centre becomes weak, and leaf production usually declines. When the clump is divided, any unhealthy-looking sections can be discarded, which allows the new plant or division to grow healthy new shoots from the rootstock around its edge.

By taking cuttings from individual plants you can produce many new plants for your herb garden. You can use a cutting to reproduce exactly the plant from which you have taken the cutting.

To take a softwood cutting, start by looking for strong and healthy new shoots as soon as the herbs begin to grow in spring. Cut them away from the parent plant with a sharp knife and, if you are taking several cuttings, put them in a plastic bag to keep them moist and cool, and to prevent them from wilting. Prepare several pots or trays with a good, well-drained cuttings compost. Make a clean cut on the stem of each cutting just below a leaf node, so that each is

10 cm (4 in) long. Cut the lower leaves off each cutting, but leave a few leaves on the stem. Make holes in the compost with a dibber, and put the cuttings in the holes up to the level of the remaining leaves.

Label each cutting with name and date, then put the pot of cuttings in a heated propagator or a mini-greenhouse made of a plastic bag. Check the cuttings daily; if using a plastic bag, take it off and turn it inside out every day.

When roots start to appear on the underside of the pot – between a fortnight and four weeks – begin to apply a foliar feed. When the plants are large enough, pot them on into individual pots. Pinch out the growing tips of leafy shoots to encourage a bushy habit.

The method for taking hardwood cuttings is similar to that for taking softwood ones, but hardwood cuttings prefer a very well-drained compost and, since they are taken later in the year – in autumn, when the stems are hard and woody – they need to be overwintered in cold frames or greenhouses before they can be planted out the following autumn. The rooting time for hardwood cuttings is much longer than for softwood cuttings.

SEQUENCE ON RIGHT **Unless they are in a very large and congested clump, chives can easily be divided by hand. Dig up and divide the clump into smaller sections by gently pulling it apart. Discard dead or damaged material. Replant smaller sections in prepared planting holes. Backfill and firm in soil at the surface. Trim the tops of the newly divided plants and water them. Keep the row weed-free and in a short time you will have a crop of fresh chives.**

A simple way to propagate or increase herbs is to take root cuttings in spring or autumn from healthy-looking plants. Mint, bergamot, lemon balm, horseradish, comfrey and sweet woodruff are among the herb plants that can be increased in this way.

Unless they are grown in crowded situations where there is no free circulation of air, or the plants are kept either too wet or too dry, herbs usually remain free of pests and diseases. It is preferable to use organic methods rather than proprietary insecticides or fungicides to deter pests from food plants such as herbs. Many organic gardeners use a proprietary organic soap to make a soapy liquid to use on whitefly or greenfly infestations. Brown spots on mint and chive

Many herbs self-seed abundantly. Others can be increased by dividing clumps, taking cuttings or sowing fresh seed in spring.

foliage are symptoms of a disease called mint or onion rust. Plants that are badly affected should be dug up and removed from the herb garden, so that other plants are not infected. You can also sterilize the soil around mint plants to prevent this disease from occurring: place a layer of straw around the affected plant and set the straw alight – but take great care to ensure that the fire does not spread.

Seedlings of basil and other herbs are prone to damping off and dying in the early stages of growth. Deterrents include good air circulation, hygienic conditions, judicious watering, and drenching the compost with a fungicidal compound before sowing.

Scale insects may be a problem on the evergreen leaves of bay grown in containers indoors. Use a soapy liquid to wipe the leaves, and dislodge the scale insects with the head of a cotton bud.

Vine weevil, whitefly and red spider mites may be persistent in protected environments, but can be controlled using soapy sprays or biological controls. Eelworms or nematodes are used for vine weevil, a parasitic wasp called *Encarsia formosa* for whitefly, and *Phytoseiulus persimilis* for red spider mites.

beautiful borders

Many of the plants categorized as herbs are attractive flowering or foliage plants that can be taken out of the context of the herb garden and used successfully in a mixed border.

Sage – whose foliage colours range from silver to purple, and include a tricolour variety that is grey-green with hints of pink and white – is a particularly effective border plant. It grows to form a low mass of coloured foliage, so it can be useful at the base of plants such as roses that may have bare stems. Later in the season, when in flower itself, sage offers extra ornament. Once the flowers are over, cut back the plant to prevent it from becoming leggy and out of shape and to encourage continuous foliage production.

If you have space to accommodate their invasive habits, herbs such as mint, comfrey and sweet Cicely will provide good-textured, colourful and shapely foliage followed by pretty flowers. All three are useful in shady sites, with mint being suited to moister conditions. Borage is another vigorous but useful foliage plant that bears eye-catching blue or white flowers in summer.

Heartsease, with its small mauve faces, is useful in containers as well as at the front of a border, winding its way through other plants. Their silver foliage and dainty pink or white scented blooms make pinks suitable for low-growing at the front of the border. Similarly, thyme will provide variegated gold or silver foliage, delicate white, mauve or pink blooms and, in some cases, a low-growing mat-like habit.

Oregano or marjoram is a rewarding herb for the middle or front of a flower border, and will grow to form quite large clumps of flowering stems in white or mauve.

ABOVE LEFT **Mauve marjoram graces the front of a border, while evening primrose, chicory and fennel offer tall stems of flowers in yellow and blue, white or (in some species of chicory) pink, which seem to float high in the air.**

BELOW LEFT **Starlike blue chicory looks lovely en masse, as well as in a mixed planting.**
RIGHT **Lavender and curry plant grow in curved shapes, which makes their silver-grey foliage useful for softening the edges of borders.**

LEFT **Echinacea, or purple coneflower, is a native American herb with a long medicinal tradition. It has many potential uses in modern medicine, and is constantly being assessed for its benefits to the human immune system. In the flower border it offers attractive long-lasting blooms late in the season.**

OPPOSITE PAGE, ABOVE **Box trained into formal shapes is a useful accent in a mixed border. Bergamot, or monarda, and marjoram bring a lovely combination of foliage and flowers to the border.**

OPPOSITE PAGE, BELOW **Pot marigolds will brighten a sunny border in spring and early summer. To encourage a continuity of flowering, remove the spent flowers before they set seed.**

Most herb flowers are in the mauve, pink or white ranges, but plants such as fennel, pot marigold, with its sunny orange and creamy yellow flowers, and nasturtium, in shades of orange, cream and red, provide great swathes of colour in the mixed border. Nasturtium has the added advantage of colourful foliage and looks good weaving its way along the front of the border. St John's wort can be used to add spots of buttery yellow to the front of the border, complementing evening primrose in a similar shade at the back; both herbs will self-seed copiously, so cut them back once the blooms are spent.

At a slightly higher level, fennel's early offering to the border is a froth of fern-like foliage in either green or bronze, followed by stiff upside-down umbrella-like flower heads with masses of small yellow dot-like flowers. These are a magnet for beneficial garden insects such as hoverflies, and, since fennel self-seeds abundantly around the garden, at the height of summer it offers great stands of colour, seemingly dancing with life.

Lavender, pinks and some other herbs grow in soft mounded shapes that spill over the border's edge. Others, such as chicory, offer flowering stems that seem to float through other plants in the border. Rosemary and bay are useful grown as standards in formal gardens, serving to raise eye-level and to make a repeated theme along a long border.

In late summer, traditional herb-garden plants, such as echinacea, or purple coneflower (also available in a white and a green form), are especially useful because they flower over a long period late in the season. Bergamot, or monarda, has a similarly long and late flowering season, and provides tall stems of flowers arranged in whorls of mauve, white and pink around its square stems. Agastache, with mauve-and-white flower spikes, is also useful for the middle of the late summer border.

covering the ground

Many low-growing herbs can be effective in the ornamental garden as ground-covering plants. Creeping thyme, for example, makes a flat green mat of foliage, and in summer offers its small mauve blooms for extra show. In a border it hugs the ground at the feet of taller plants, suppressing weeds and providing its own colour. Deadhead thyme after flowering, using shears or clippers. Remove any weed seedlings that grow through the ground cover and water it in dry spells.

Since it supports light trampling underfoot, thyme can be used for a short path. More formally, it makes a witty and attractive feature if planted in a circle at the base of a sundial. You can also use a slightly taller thyme for an inner circle within the creeping thyme outer circle, adding contrast to the colour and texture of the ground cover.

Creeping chamomile is also useful as a fragrant ground cover, to create an aromatic lawn or as a pathway plant. Remove all perennial weeds and any stones from the soil before planting. For 1 square metre (1 square yard), you will need 40 individual chamomile plants. Water the plants in well, and avoid walking on the path or lawn until they are well established and have meshed together.

Either thyme or chamomile makes a fragrant cover for a turf seat or bench. Site the seat against an existing wall and make a back for it with trellis or wood. You can build up the seat in front of it as you would a raised bed, using smaller raised beds to form the 'arms' of the seat. Plant the creeping herbs in the soil within the various raised areas and, if you are using trellis for the back, plant a climber such as jasmine into the bed, for fragrance in the air and at your back.

Prostrate rosemary, although it is slower growing than thyme and chamomile, and also tender in cold areas, is effective both as a ground cover and trailing over the edges of beds. Plant in full sun.

Corsican mint, *Mentha requienii*, won't support feet, but it does make a good cover at the edge of a pond or in a moist, shady conditions. Similarly, creeping mint, *M. pulegium*, is attractive in a shady, slightly damp area of the garden. Herbs such as *Alchemilla mollis*, sweet Cicely and salad burnet, although not ground-hugging, are useful ground-cover plants in a large garden. As they self-seed abundantly, their spread can be prodigious.

LEFT Two types of thyme form the ground cover that frames pots holding lemon verbena and an ornamental garden plant, Perovskia 'Blue Spire'.

ABOVE AND RIGHT Creeping thyme (above) or chamomile (right) wears better when grown in between stepping stones. Either herb supports light traffic and provides a highly aromatic pathway to a bench or an arbour. Both need clipping back to stop them covering the stepping stones.

a hedge of herbs

Rosemary, thyme, santolina, box and lavender are among the herbs that can be grown as shaped low hedges to enclose formal features or even to form the fabric of herb parterres. Herb hedges are usually shaped to make linear ribbons of foliage that outline or emphasize special areas of a herb garden. Yew may be slow-growing, but once it is established it is a very elegant dark-green foil for herbs, and in the general garden it is particularly useful as an architectural hedge plant.

Knot gardens and parterres are the usual formal features created with herb plants. The colour of the hedge depends on the plants you choose for it. For a silvery effect, use lavender or santolina or even curry plant. Thyme, rosemary and box provide green elements, and by mixing the silver and greens you can create a woven effect.

Although you can achieve a formal effect by keeping lavender closely clipped, you can also create a relaxed and informal look by

OPPOSITE PAGE **A circle of wall germander, or *Teucrium chamaedrys*, is created from single plants of the same size planted to a particular design then cut back annually to form the desired shape.**

RIGHT **Cotton lavender or santolina can be grown to achieve a silvery effect.**

BELOW LEFT **After it has finished flowering, cut back the lavender to a uniform height for a fragrant hedge.**

allowing it to flower in summer, then cutting it back once the flowering is finished. A lavender hedge makes an attractive feature on either side of a pathway, but remember to make the path wide enough to allow the lavender spikes to spill across it and yet leave enough space for you to walk along.

In a vegetable garden use parsley, wild strawberries or chives to edge part of the garden. This will provide an informal and semi-permanent hedge, which will alter as you harvest from it.

When you plant a herb hedge use plants of the same height and size so that you achieve a uniform look more quickly. Plant box or yew into individual planting holes along a line of string. Water the plants in well and, if necessary, provide a temporary windbreak of hessian to help the young plants survive in their first winter.

When the hedge is well established, you can begin to clip it to maintain it. Cut back knot-garden or parterre hedges in early autumn, so that there is time for them to recover before the cold weather sets in. Woody plants such as sage, thyme, lavender and rosemary should be cut back to half the year's growth to promote bushy shapes. For extra effect, cut special shapes, such as triangles, globes or even whimsical animals or birds, into the hedges.

herbs in the kitchen garden

Growing popular culinary herbs such as parsley and chives as crops in the vegetable garden means you can harvest from several plants at the same time rather than from one or two – so that each plant loses some of its foliage, flowers or seeds, but enough remains for the plant to continue to be decorative and viable.

Group tall-growing plants such as fennel and lovage together and plant them at the back of the vegetable garden so that they don't cast shade on or take light away from lower-growing herbs. Low-growing herbs such as parsley, salad burnet, chives and buckler leaf sorrel look attractive in short rows in raised beds.

Sow parsley in succession through the summer so that you have a number of rows at different stages. Once parsley begins to send up a strong, tough flowering stem its foliage becomes less aromatic, and you should uproot the plants. If you have an informal vegetable garden, allow one to flower and set seed, and then to self-seed.

Summer savory, an annual with tasty edible flowers and foliage, has traditionally been cooked and served with broad beans; it is also often used as a companion plant for broad beans in the vegetable garden. Another good companion herb is sweet Cicely, traditionally linked with one of the early fruits of the productive garden, rhubarb. Use its leafy shoots to sweeten and reduce the acidity of rhubarb. Sweet Cicely self-sows copiously, so remove its seeds once they have formed or harvest them to use as aniseed-flavoured sweets.

Mint is an invaluable kitchen herb, useful in salads and in cooked dishes, sauces and jams and jellies. It is a vigorous plant, and is best grown in containers sunk into the ground, or in a section of the vegetable garden that can be cordoned off from the rest of the rows. Although its flowers are attractive, keep cutting out flowering stems to encourage more leafy shoots.

Cut back thyme and sage after flowering to promote the growth of new leafy shoots. Rosemary also benefits from cutting back. Some woody herbs become leggy and unshapely in time. If this happens, replace them with new plants.

Grow golden marjoram and chervil in relative shade in the vegetable garden. Chervil is a biennial producing leafy growth in its first year, so make successive sowings to keep your kitchen supplied with its subtle flavours.

Herbs such as nasturtium, heartsease and pot marigold provide edible flowers for use in salads. Chive flower heads are also good in salads – pick them just as the buds begin to open.

OPPOSITE PAGE, TOP ROW
Confine vigorous mint (left) in a restricted area of the kitchen garden. Rosemary (centre) can be clipped into shapes or allowed to grow freely. Use flat-leaved parsley (right) as a seasonal edging.

OPPOSITE PAGE, BOTTOM ROW
Harvest the aromatic seeds of caraway (left) after the flowers die back. Mossy curly-leaved parsley (centre) can also be used as a temporary edging. The flowers, foliage and seeds of nasturtium (right) are spicy in food – and it will romp through the vegetable garden, providing annual colour.

Shrubby herbs such as rosemary, sage and thyme need extra space in the vegetable garden, but you are unlikely to need more than one or two of each to support your cooking needs.

creating a herb collection

If you have space to grow herbs for ornament, display them in groups according to their use or to show the differences between plants in the same genus. There are herbs for every theme and colour scheme. For example, collections of mint, rosemary, thyme, sage, lavender and marjoram reveal a wide range of foliage colour, flower colour and, in many cases, essential oils and aromas. Such collections, arranged by genus and species, show the characteristics of the various plants and display the differences between each species and form.

Before you plant a collection you need to know the maximum heights and spreads of the various plants and how much sun they need. Look at the different foliage colours and place them so that they look good together.

The simplest collection consists of the herbs you use often in the kitchen. Grow them in a small circular bed or in containers close to the kitchen door, for easy access. You could devote a small rectangular bed to bay, thyme and parsley, the three classic herbs of a *bouquet*

ABOVE **Mints are best grown in individual pots to prevent these vigorous plants from overwhelming each other.**

LEFT **Rosemary flowers can be white, pink, mauve or blue. Most species are medium-height, but 'Miss Jessopp's Upright', which can grow to 2.5 m (8 ft), needs to be carefully sited in such a collection, as does prostrate or creeping rosemary.**

RIGHT AND OPPOSITE PAGE **A circle is a popular shape for a basic culinary collection containing herbs such as rosemary, chives, marjoram and buckler leaf sorrel.**

garni. Choose a standard or conical-shaped bay as the central focus. Plant thyme bushes in the corners of the bed, and fill the centre with parsley. For a *fines herbes* collection, grow parsley, chervil, chives and tarragon. If you like Italian cuisine, grow bay, basil, marjoram, garlic, rosemary and sage. For an Asian taste, choose coriander, lemon grass, Japanese parsley, perilla and mint. Pizza herb gardens containing marjoram, basil, basil and rosemary are popular in the USA.

You could also group together herbs whose leaves are used dried or fresh to make teas and tisanes, such as sage, mint, bergamot and chamomile. Other possibilities include fragrant herbs for a potpourri collection, and an edible flower collection. Enjoy cowslip and violet flowers crystallized or baked in cakes and scones. Use pot marigold, chive and thyme flowers fresh in salads. Lavender flowers and rose petals added to ordinary or caster sugar will transform it into a scented sweetener for baking and desserts.

The many herbs that have citrus-scented foliage would make an attractive collection with their differing heights, shapes, foliage and flower colours. Such plants include variegated lemon balm, lemon verbena, lemon thyme and some tender herbs such as lemon-scented basil, lemon grass and *Eucalyptus citriodora*.

LEFT **A number of different thyme species are grown within a small parterre or knot garden, hedged in by rosemary, box and a golden form of the honeysuckle Lonicera nitida, 'Baggessen's Gold', a shrubby hedge plant.**

RIGHT **Edging an informal path with collections of marjoram and catmint offers a flowing, curving shape to the garden and displays differences in flower colour.**

herbs in containers

Many low-growing or trailing herbs grow well in containers, and containers make it easy to ring the changes and replace spent herbs quickly as you use particular plants or different varieties become available during the season.

The most convenient containers for kitchen herbs are window boxes placed just outside the kitchen, so that you can harvest foliage and flowers easily and quickly without having to step outside, or large ground-level containers on a patio.

If any of the herbs in a container dies, or you harvest them so completely that they are no longer attractive, it is simple to remove and replace them. In addition, if you are going to be using and replacing the herbs regularly, you can leave them in their individual containers, all set into a sturdy wooden window box, with the box becoming a cachepot for the various smaller containers. You can replace any herb that is not growing well without having to replant the whole box.

There is a range of different containers that are suitable for herb growing. Terracotta and plastic are popular choices, but you can use almost anything, from large olive-oil cans to half-barrels, to create a particular style and house your herb collection.

There are two things you need to be sure of when planting up a container with herbs. First, it should have a depth of at least 25–30 cm (10–12 in), to give the roots adequate space to make strong root runs. Second, larger containers are heavy to move once they are filled with moist compost, so you need to site them carefully before you plant

LEFT **Terracotta pots are attractive containers for herbs because they weather so well. Annual herbs and some perennials, including chives, thrive in small pots in the short term. Woody perennials such as sage and thyme need relatively deep pots so that their roots can get properly established.**

them up. If you are planting up a window box or hanging basket, make sure that it is securely fixed in position. When it is full of moist soil it will be very heavy, and if it became unsecured it could fall and hurt someone passing underneath it, especially if you happen to live in an apartment.

Remove the individual herbs from their pots and place them on a drainage layer of broken terracotta and a layer of soil-based compost. Fill the spaces between the herbs with compost and firm the plants in with your hands. Water the soil and cover its surface with a layer of grit to hold the compost in place and to act as a water-absorbent mulch.

There are a number of herbs that will thrive growing together in a container in a sunny situation. Avoid tall-growing plants – especially for a window box where the window opens outwards – because they will flop over the edge and may be damaged by wind.

Low-growing or trailing herbs and stately standards make a fine display in containers.

ABOVE **Thyme and sage combine well in a basket with ornamental flowering plants such as trailing verbena.**
BELOW AND BELOW RIGHT **Weathered stone sinks or sculpted terracotta** pots are practical and attractive containers for shrubby herbs such as sage. They are also suitable for low-growing collections of creeping and upright thymes.

LEFT **Standard bay trees make strong focal points in a formal herb garden. In winter, insulate the pot with bubble wrap to prevent frost damage and stablize it so that it doesn't blow over.**

OPPOSITE PAGE **A bold and flamboyant display in a container can be used as a marker for the meeting point of paths or to provide a change of height in the low-growing herb garden.**

growing herbs indoors

Many herbs can be grown indoors all year round, but indoor herbs are particularly useful in winter for quick harvesting. In sheltered sites they can also be grown on patios and balconies throughout the winter.

It is advisable to treat indoor herbs as practical or useful plants with short shelf or windowsill lives rather than as long-lived plants. In common with other container-grown plants, they need nutrients, water, protection from pests, adequate light and free circulation of air.

A kitchen windowsill is usually the most suitable site for herbs in pots because it is convenient for the cook and is likely to have good light and air circulation. Choose attractive containers for extra decorative effect, or group together several herbs in larger containers to create a mini-herb garden indoors.

As a general rule, herbs should be grown in separate pots in well-drained compost. This allows easy replacement of dead or overharvested herbs. Water the plants regularly, but in winter keep rosemary, sage, winter savory and thyme just moist.

Herbs grown indoors in summer need a liquid feed every two to three weeks – or add a slow-release fertilizer pellet to the compost when you pot the plants up. Use a spray of insecticidal soap to kill off any whitefly; spray every 14 days until the infestation has abated.

Harvest from the herbs as required, but turn each plant around every few days to encourage even leafy growth and to help you to harvest evenly from it. If you overharvest from one plant it will look less attractive and may become more vulnerable to pests and diseases. For quick results, replace indoor plants with new ones bought from supermarkets; for a longer growing period, replace them with herbs from garden centres. You can sow parsley and chervil in succession to provide new material.

Evergreen herbs such as rosemary, sage and thyme grow well indoors. Annuals such as basil and parsley last for a short time, but replacement pots can be bought regularly from supermarkets for immediate use.

If you have no garden and are growing herbs in pots indoors all year round, repot evergreen perennials annually in spring. The plants may need replacing every two or three years. Plants such as fennel

Herbs in the kitchen are a boon to the cook, but they need a light and airy site to thrive.

and dill, which would normally grow very tall outdoors, should be harvested when they are reasonably short, or the plant will become leggy and look untidy and out of line with its windowsill companions.

If you have a heated greenhouse, you can force tarragon, mint and chives into growing during what is normally their dormant season. Pot them up in autumn and keep them in the greenhouse through the winter, planting them out into the garden in spring.

Container herbs can be bought from supermarkets at any time of the year to fill the flavour gap between your own sowings and provide leaves for salads and cooked dishes. The hot-house conditions in which they are grown are difficult to replicate in the average draughty kitchen, but you can prolong their lives by keeping them out of draughts, watering them from the base and harvesting them evenly. Even if you are careful with them, it is unlikely that supermarket plants will become long-term inhabitants of your indoor collection. In some circles they are known as 'cut-and-chuck' herbs because of their short-term use.

Supermarkets can also be a source of unusual herbs for indoors. For example, lemon grass plants can be grown from stems bought in supermarket packs. (In some Oriental supermarkets they are sold loose.) Choose the plumpest stem and check that it has not been sliced at the base. Plant the stem into a gritty compost and keep it on the dry side during winter. Alternatively, good-sized plants are available from specialist herb growers and will provide citrus-scented foliage much earlier than the supermarket stems.

LEFT **Fennel, parsley, basil and sage will grow well on a sunny windowsill but should be kept out of draughts. Fennel tends to become leggy if grown indoors in a container, so use it quickly.**

living with herbs

To create a warm welcome, bring the essence of a summer garden indoors with a potpourri of flowers, herbs and spices.

The original 'rotten pot' that gave us the word potpourri was a wet mixture of fermented petals and leaves. Today, the dry potpourri is more popular. Its scent may not last as long as that of the moist variety, but the combinations of textures, colours and aromas are endless. The basic ingredients are flowers for scent or colour, aromatic leaves, peel and spices, and a fixative – usually powdered orris root – to preserve the blend. Use 1 tablespoon of orris root for each cupped handful of dried flowers and leaves; then add a few drops of essential oils, if desired.

ABOVE AND OPPOSITE PAGE **For a zesty hallway, add essential oils of bergamot, grapefruit and lemon to a bowl of dried lemon balm, lemon verbena, mint, yellow rosebuds and citrus slices. Any essential oil must be used sparingly or it will drown the subtler scents of the leaves and petals. The potpourri in this shallow bowl – about the size of a standard dinner plate – needs no more than 2 drops of each oil.**

RIGHT **If you want to enhance the rustic feel in a room with plenty of wooden furniture, mix 2 or 3 drops of essential oils of pine, sandalwood and cedar with large handfuls of dried rose petals, bay leaves and lavender sprigs, along with generous sprinklings of ground cinnamon and nutmeg.**

Designed for comfort and entertaining, living rooms are full of soft furnishings and display surfaces that offer a host of opportunities for scenting and decorating with herbs.

A simple way to scent your home is to have arrangements of fresh flowers and herbs in every room, but there are other, more imaginative ways to keep it smelling delicious and inviting all year round.

For example, herb sachets – which have traditionally been used to freshen drawers and linen cupboards – can also be tucked into cushions, into the pockets of everyday coats and clothes, and down the sides of comfy chairs and sofas. Fragrances are released when herb-filled cushions are pressed or leant against; curtain hems can be filled with dried aromatic herbs, or fresh lavender sprigs can simply be tucked into muslin curtains. Experiment with different mixtures of dried herbs and essential oils to make a potpourri, perhaps combining it with a pomander. Circulating air will pick up and mingle these scents, so ensure that the various fragrances are complementary, and there is no clash of pungent odours.

For a sweet aroma, choose from herbs that sweeten, which include bay, lavender, lemon verbena, rosemary, santolina, myrtle, thyme and sweet woodruff.

ABOVE LEFT AND OPPOSITE PAGE **Herb sachets can be a decorative element in themselves, while subtly perfuming an entire room – the perfect setting in which to enjoy a cup of chamomile tea.**

ABOVE RIGHT **For a heady, long-lasting winter fragrance, press cloves into oranges to make pomanders. Display several in a dish with a selection of herbs and spices such as bay, eucalyptus, juniper berries and cinnamon.**

Pocketing a subtle perfume

A pocket in a cushion invites you to fill it with herbs. Herbs that are good for this purpose include eucalyptus (opposite page), rosemary and bay leaves. For a mixture of herbs, whole or crushed, cut a square of muslin and fold it to make an envelope around the herbs (this page). Wrap a band of linen around a cushion, securing the ends with a button or a stitch. Tuck the folded muslin sachet under the band. Essential oils sprinkled on the muslin bag enhance and prolong the fragrance.

BELOW You can buy ready-scented beeswax candles, or add essential oils or small pieces of dried herb to melted beeswax while making your own. Tied up in ribbon with lavender sprigs, these make beautiful home-made Christmas presents.

A handful of woody sprigs on a log fire sweetens the smoky aromas of winter.

ABOVE AND LEFT If you have a log fire, throw on a handful of woody-stemmed herbs every so often to release the rich aromas. Layering logs with branches of rosemary both looks pretty and complements the woody smells.

Burning woody herbs such as rosemary, lavender and bay will fill a room with rich musty aromas. Either keep a box of dried herbs by an open fire to use as kindling, or throw an occasional handful on the embers. Logs stored in the home can be layered with generous sprigs of rosemary (drying the rosemary beforehand should stop it going black).

Another delicious winter fragrance is the smell of burning candles. To create your own herbal version, buy a candlemaking kit. Just before pouring the melted wax into moulds, add small pieces of dried herb, such as bergamot, wall germander, lavender heads, lemon thyme, mint, rosemary or myrtle, or a few drops of essential oil of your choice.

A flamboyant winter wreath creates a Yuletide mood.

One of the most traditional ways of using herbs for decoration is to weave them into a wreath. This adds fragrance and colour to a room and, if used imaginatively, can become the central focus. The wreath shown is a strong enough statement to be the only festive decoration in the room.

To make a wreath, use plain wire, moss-covered wire or willow, and secure into a hoop. (Or buy a hoop ready-made at any florist's shop.) Using thin wire, attach bunches of selected herbs. For the main body of the wreath, use branches of pine, eucalyptus, bay and rosemary, then carefully tuck in among the branches slices of dried oranges, lemons and limes, fresh or dried Chinese lanterns and bundles of cinnamon sticks. For the final festive touch, add bunches of red berries.

If the wreath is to hang horizontally, attach it to a strong structure such as the iron candelabra illustrated. When it is time to take down the wreath, burn the bunches of herbs on an open fire and enjoy the powerful aroma.

LEFT AND RIGHT **A wreath of pine branches, eucalyptus, rosemary, bay, slices of dried citrus fruit, and bundles of cinnamon sticks will fill a room with a distinctively festive mixture of colours, textures and fragrances.**

Generous bunches of dried herbs, or herbs preserved in attractive bottles of oil or vinegar, can be used in the kitchen for decorative as well as culinary purposes.

The medieval still room for processing and preserving herbs has long since disappeared from the home. Such activities are now likely to take place in the kitchen, where herbs may also be stored, grown (see pages 54–55) or – as in other rooms – used decoratively.

As soon as possible after harvesting or buying herbs, put them in water and out of direct sunlight. To revive cooking herbs that are starting to wilt, put them in a plastic bag filled with air and secure it tightly; stored in the refrigerator, they should last a few extra days.

The sooner after harvesting that the drying process begins the better the quality and colour of the dried herbs, but drying cannot be rushed because moisture must be removed gradually from a plant. Wipe off any soil or grit but avoid washing the leaves. Choose a warm,

dry, dark place with good ventilation, such as an airing cupboard or a heated loft or attic. Hang several sprigs of each herb in separate small bunches, tied loosely with string or raffia, so that the air can get in and around each bunch. Leave herbs hanging, stems upwards, for about a week, until the leaves are paper-dry and fragile but not disintegrating. Remove leaves from stems, keeping them whole, and store in airtight bottles away from sunlight. Check dried leaves regularly for moisture, mould and insects, and throw them away if you find anything wrong. Most dried herbs will last for about a year.

Freezing is a good way to retain the colour and flavour of delicate herbs such as basil, chives, dill and tarragon. Before freezing, wipe the herbs and pack them into labelled plastic food bags or boxes.

ABOVE LEFT **To dry herbs, tie a few sprigs together and hang them in a warm, dark room.**
ABOVE **Herb oils and vinegars should be stored in airtight bottles out of direct sunlight.**

RIGHT **Hanging herbs from the ceiling can produce a dramatic decorative effect. Bunches of sage, lemon balm, rosemary and eucalyptus, dried or fresh, will brighten up any kitchen.**

RIGHT The acrid smell of rue repels flies and ants. Hang up bunches of the herb in utility rooms to discourage infestations, and press the leaves occasionally to release their pungent scent.

BELOW Pretty posies of santolina in your linen drawers will ward off the dreaded moth.

LEFT **To give a wonderfully fresh fragrance to floors and surfaces, clean them with 6 drops of an essential oil added to 2 litres of warm water. Choose from oils of lemon, tea tree, thyme, lavender, sandalwood, peppermint and eucalyptus.**

RIGHT **To make your wooden furniture smell dreamy, add a few drops of essential oil of lavender to a good-quality beeswax furniture polish, and apply with a clean dry cloth.**

Herbs have always had an important practical role in the household, and that remains true today – indeed, incorporating herbs or essential herbal oils in your cleaning routine can make household chores an aromatic pleasure. You can use them to disinfect floors and surfaces, to repel unwanted visitors such as moths and other insects, and to sweeten and purify stale, musty air.

Ants are seen off by sprigs of pennyroyal, rue and tansy left on larder shelves. Rue also deters flies, as do lavender, mint, mugwort, pennyroyal and peppermint. Use the herbs dried in potpourri, or fresh in arrangements and wreaths. Make sure that the leaves are disturbed occasionally to release more scent. To prevent unwelcome visits from weevils, place a few bay leaves in bins of flour, rice and dried pulses.

Herbal preparations have a multitude of practical uses in the home – and they are frequently kinder to your skin and the environment than chemical-based cleaners.

ABOVE Roses, pelargoniums and Chinese lanterns add colour to a summer garland of flat-leaved parsley, bay, lemon balm, coriander, fennel, apple mint, eucalyptus and sage.

RIGHT As well as making flamboyant centrepieces, fresh herbs can be used for plate decorations, in finger bowls and in place-marker pots.

FAR RIGHT Leaves of borage and mint with cucumber slices make iced water even more refreshing. Coriander flowers impart a delicate flavour to pepper and salt.

Decorating a summer table with fresh herbs is a joy in itself. There is such a wide choice of plants and flowers available in summer that each detail can be a celebration of a different herb. For example, wrapping flowering rosemary around napkins will encourage your guests to appreciate the plant's delicate purple flower.

For your tablecloth, choose a pale natural fabric such as undyed linen. This will allow the herbs to hold centre stage rather than making them compete with a busy pattern. Height is important in any table setting, and one easy way to achieve it is to decorate candlesticks or candelabra. Soak a foam brick in water. (These can be bought in any florist's shop and, if kept damp, will maintain the freshness of the the herbs for days.) Slice off two chunks, one for each side of the candlestick, and use florist's tape to wrap them together. Rosemary, eucalyptus, lemon balm, parsley, flowering apple mint and various

Intensify the pleasures of summer dining by combining the delicate scents of freshly cut flowers and herbs with the stronger aromas of herbs used in cookery and the spicy flavours of salad herbs.

Each place setting is adorned with a herbal napkin ring, a finger bowl sprinkled with aromatic herbs and a miniature pot of herbs that acts as a holder for guest name-tags.

pelargoniums make a good base. You can then introduce more delicate herbs and flowers such as flowering coriander and old-fashioned scented roses. Combining culinary herbs and scent-giving herbs in a table decoration can produce very satisfying results, especially if the culinary herbs have also been used in the preparation of food.

As with the tablecloth, choose plain or understated china, cutlery and glassware that will not upstage the greenery. Arrange the herbs loosely; think about how they grow in the garden and let them ramble across the table. Herbs wilt quickly, so make sure they are in plenty of water. Spray loose herbs with water half an hour before your guests sit down, to keep the table looking fresh.

OPPOSITE PAGE, LEFT **A sprig of rosemary tied loosely around a crisp linen napkin is a pretty alternative to a napkin ring.**

OPPOSITE PAGE, RIGHT **The woody stems of lemon balm are easily woven into lattice-pattern place mats. When a hot plate is placed on a mat, a delicious aroma is released.**

ABOVE **Float mint and lemon balm in small glass bowls of water to give your visitors a pleasant way to freshen their fingers between courses.**

ABOVE RIGHT **Write the names of your guests on copper plant tags and put them into miniature terracotta plant pots filled with fresh herbs.**

A bowl of freshly torn herbs such as basil, mint, tarragon, coriander and flat-leaved parsley is an attractive detail – and guests can help themselves to handfuls to sprinkle on their food.

If you have a conservatory to dine in, or if your dining room is full of natural light, take advantage of this environment to grow herbs in containers (see pages 54–55). Surround the table with pots of delicious-smelling culinary and aromatic herbs. For containers that are intended to be a permanent feature, choose unusual items such as china basins and chimney pots. Trailing herbs in hanging baskets make romantic decorations; suitable varieties include prostrate rosemary, prostrate sage, creeping thymes, catmint and the colourful nasturtium.

Although they may seem out of place in an office, herbs can do much to enhance your working environment. Particular varieties invigorate and uplift the mind, aiding concentration and inspiration. Keep a pot of fresh herbs on your desk or near your work area, where the leaves and flowers will be lovely to look at and will gently fragrance the air.

Essential oils sprinkled onto a tissue or handkerchief are an alternative to fresh herbs and provide a stronger herbal 'hit'. Basil is energizing and invigorating and is used to treat depression. Coriander and eucalpytus are also uplifting. Geranium is refreshing and relaxing, as is lavender. Lemon balm bursts with zingy fragrance, and thyme is good for combating depression and fatigue.

Even the paper you use can be scented – either buy it ready-scented or add a few drops of essential oil. Stick dried herbs to paper or leave them loose in a folded letter. A sophisticated flower press is not needed. Simply take a perfect flower or leaf and sandwich it between two piles of blotting or watercolour paper. Put this sandwich between the leaves of a large heavy book and pile three or four more heavy books on top of it. Leave for a couple of weeks, until the herbs have dried out.

Ink too can be fragranced. Immerse 25 g of dried aromatic flowers (such as myrtle, lavender flowers, lemon verbena, pelargonium or rosemary) in water and bring to the boil. Simmer for 30–40 minutes until it has reduced to 4 tsp of pungent dark liquid. Strain, allow to cool and add to a bottle of ordinary ink.

ABOVE **As a powerful aid to concentration, place a jugful of fresh herbs such as basil and mint on a desk or elsewhere in a work space.**

RIGHT **Writing paper can be scented with a few drops of essential oil and decorated with dried pressed herbs. Even the ink you use to write a letter can be fragranced.**

Refreshing and
invigorating herbs
can bring a new
sense of purpose
to your working
space, and revive
some of the almost
forgotten pleasures
of letter writing.

LEFT **Herbs with colourful and pretty blooms can be dried and pressed in the same way as any wild flowers before being incorporated into eye-catching arrangements.**

Fragrant nosegays and tussie-mussies were traditionally associated with declarations of love or used to ward off dangerous diseases.

LEFT **This tussie-mussie includes flowering thyme for courage, fennel for strength, lemon balm for sympathy and geranium for comfort.**

RIGHT **A bridal bed decorated with fresh flowering thyme, rosemary, pelargoniums, eucalyptus and roses looks romantic and will fill a room with fresh summer smells.**

Nosegays or tussie-mussies – posies made up of aromatic herbs and flowers – were popular from medieval times not only because of their ability to disguise unlovely smells but also because they were thought to protect the holder from disease. They were also used for declarations of love, since all the flowers and herbs had special meanings. A lover might send a posy of, for example, mint for virtue, forget-me-nots for true love, golden marjoram for blushes, myrtle for love, rosemary for remembrance and ivy for fidelity. Guests will be sure to appreciate such a posy placed on a pillow or at the bedside, even if they have no idea of the signficance of the herbs and flowers used.

To fill a bedroom with summer scent in winter, spray bed linen with a fresh linen spray or sprinkle pillows with a diluted essential oil. Chamomile, lavender, lemon balm and oregano promote sound sleep.

Garlanded with scent

ABOVE **Catmint's long woody stems are easy to loop into a fresh herbal garland.**

ABOVE RIGHT **Its strength and pliability make dried lavender ideal for bending and weaving into shape.**

To scent a room in winter, when fresh herbs are scarce, you can vaporize an essential herbal oil in a ceramic burner. Add a few drops of oil to water in the bowl and use a nightlight to heat it gently from beneath.

Garlands serve the same purpose as potpourris. They are designed to scent the air and the objects around them, but in a more decorative way. They can be hung on the backs of doors and the corners of beds,

or simply placed on a pillow to welcome a guest. Only herbs with tough and pliable stems can be used to make garlands because they must be able to withstand being looped and twisted. For fresh herbal garlands use catmint, lemon balm, lemon verbena, marjorams, mints and scented pelargoniums. Rosemary, lavender, bay, myrtle and eucalpytus are rewarding to use in either fresh or dried form.

THIS PAGE The scent of lavender has a relaxing effect and promotes sound sleep, so it is a particularly appropriate herb for decorative use in the bedroom.

ABOVE **Put a bar of herbal soap on a bed of fresh mint. An invigorating aroma is released when the leaves are gently crushed.**

ABOVE CENTRE **Fresh herbs can be suspended from the hot tap before the bath is filled with water. Lemon balm and eucalyptus, for example, have a wonderfully revitalizing effect in the morning.**

LEFT AND ABOVE RIGHT **Scatter lavender around the bath and put down a cotton mat to stand on. The scent of crushed herb fills the bathroom and permeates nearby rooms.**

An aromatic herbal bath is one of the most pleasurable ways to cleanse your skin and revitalize your whole body. You can add particular herbs to promote relaxation or stimulation.

Some herbs invigorate; others soothe the mind and body, promoting peaceful sleep. For stimulation, choose basil, bay, eucalyptus, lemon verbena, mint, rosemary, sage and thyme. For relaxation, the preferred herbs are chamomile, lavender and lemon balm.

To treat minor skin irritations or soothe dry sensitive skin, use calendula, comfrey, fennel, lady's mantle, parsley and spearmint.

Any of these herbs can be used, in dried form, in a herbal bath. The herbs should be crushed or ground and put into a muslin bag; hang the bag under a hot running tap.

The water in a herbal bath should be close to body temperature; if it is too hot, the skin perspires and fails to take advantage of the therapeutic qualities. To enjoy the full benefits of the bath, wallow in it for at least 10 minutes.

Therapeutic preparations can be made at home from essential oils and herbal infusions.

lavender spritz

For a classic skin freshener, fill an atomizer bottle with distilled water and add a couple of drops of lavender oil. Shake to blend.

hand cream

225 ml rosewater
60 ml cornflour
60 ml glycerine
3 drops chamomile oil

Blend rosewater, glycerine and cornflour. Heat gently in a double saucepan to thicken, then cool. Stir in oil. Store in screw-top jar.

lip balm

Oil of eucalyptus, lemon, thyme, jasmine, lavender, geranium, juniper or peppermint

Add 2 drops of the oil of your choice to 1 tbspn of warmed cocoa butter. Scoop into a small screw-top jar and allow to cool.

rosewater toner

160 ml rosewater
150 ml witch hazel
6 drops glycerine

Pour all the ingredients into a bottle and shake well before use.

vinegar bath

Boil leaves of lemon balm and pennyroyal in cider vinegar. Infuse overnight, then strain. Pour into warm water for a refreshing bath.

massage oil

5 drops lavender oil
5 drops neroli oil
6 drops frankincense
50 ml almond oil

Add oils to a small stoppered jar and shake to blend. Massage gently into the skin to firm it up and to combat stretch marks.

foot bath

Fresh leaves of bay, eucalyptus, lavender, lemon balm, thyme, marjoram, spearmint

Sprinkle handfuls of herbs into a large bowl. Add 2 teaspoons of salt and enough hot water to cover the feet and ankles. Soak feet for at least 10 minutes while breathing in the delicious aroma.

antiseptic wash

Among oils with antiseptic action are thyme, lavender, tea tree and eucalyptus. Add 8 drops of one of these to a small bowl of water and apply to minor wounds.

Essential oils should not be used undiluted, nor taken internally except on medical advice.

Essential herbal oils or fresh herbs steeped in hot water can be used to create a wide variety of bathroom tonics – or simply to enhance the luxury of bathing.

cooking with herbs

vinegars, dressings, oils and butters

Vinegars and dressings take on a slightly exotic flavour when combined with herbs, and there are many herbs that are good for this purpose. Flavoured vinegars enhance fruit syrups and salad dressings – or can be used to deglaze a pan in which meat or fish has been fried.

tarragon vinegar

2 sprigs of tarragon (or thyme, lavender or chives)
500 ml white wine vinegar

Makes 500 ml

Put the herb in the vinegar and leave in a warm sunny place for 3–4 days to let the flavour develop. Use as required.

tarragon vinegar dressing

1 tablespoon tarragon vinegar
4 tablespoons hazelnut oil
2 tablespoons extra virgin olive oil
½ teaspoon caster sugar
sea salt and freshly ground black pepper

Make the tarragon vinegar as described above. Then mix all the ingredients and use as required.

mixed herb dressing

The different combinations of herbs that can be used to make this dressing are virtually endless.

2 tablespoons chopped mixed herbs: basil, chervil, chives, parsley and mint
125 ml extra virgin olive oil
1 tablespoon good-quality balsamic vinegar
1 tablespoon Dijon mustard
1 garlic clove, lightly crushed
sea salt and freshly ground black pepper

Makes 150 ml

Whisk the chopped herbs into the olive oil. Beat in the vinegar and mustard. Season to taste, then add the garlic clove.

Use the dressing once or store it in the refrigerator for up to 2 days. Return it to room temperature before use.

coriander, soy and sesame dressing

As well as giving a refreshing zing to hearty vegetable salads, this dressing is delicious trickled over grilled chicken or pan-grilled and sliced duck breast.

2 tablespoons chopped coriander
1 tablespoon dark soy sauce
1 teaspoon clear honey
1 teaspoon wholegrain mustard
2 teaspoons rice vinegar
1 tablespoon sesame oil
5 tablespoons peanut oil

Makes 125 ml

Whisk all the ingredients together and use as required.

basil oil

You can easily enhance the flavour of a tomato salad and add colour contrast by tossing it gently in basil oil.

25 g fresh basil (or parsley)
*   leaves*
300 ml extra virgin olive oil
a pinch of sea salt

Makes about 200 ml

Put the basil leaves, oil and salt in a food processor and blend to make a vivid green paste. Infuse overnight, then strain the oil through a layer of muslin.

Use the oil as required or store it in a refrigerator. Return it to room temperature before use.

thyme, lemon and chilli oil

For a quick and delicious supper, toss cooked pasta in a good dash of the oil; top with sautéed mushrooms and a sprinkling of freshly grated Pecorino cheese.

4 sprigs of thyme
4 pieces of lemon zest,
*   cut into thin strips*
2 small red chillies, finely sliced
600 ml extra virgin olive oil

Makes about 600 ml

Put the thyme, lemon strips and sliced chillies in a bottle and add the oil. Infuse for 7–10 days, then strain into a clean bottle.

fragrant Thai oil

This subtly spiced oil is wonderful trickled over steamed fish or added to marinades.

2 stalks of lemon grass,
*   halved lengthways*
6 kaffir lime leaves or lime zest
2 slices of galangal or root
*   ginger*
1 bird's eye chilli
600 ml sunflower oil

Makes about 600 ml

Lightly crush the herbs and aromatics and put them in a wide-necked bottle. Top up with the sunflower oil.

Leave to infuse for 7–10 days in a cool place before using.

rosemary, garlic and pepper oil

To savour the delights of this pungently aromatic oil, use it as a dip for focaccia or ciabatta bread. An alternative is to trickle it over a freshly baked pizza (see page 98).

4 sprigs of rosemary
2 garlic cloves, sliced
1 tablespoon black peppercorns,
*   lightly crushed*
600 ml extra virgin olive oil

Makes about 600 ml

Put the rosemary, sliced garlic and peppercorns in a small saucepan with the olive oil. Heat gently until just boiling and simmer for 1 minute. Let cool, then infuse overnight.

The following day, strain the infused oil into a clean bottle and add a sprig of rosemary and a few whole black peppercorns for decoration.

Combining herbs and oils is a terrific way both to preserve the herbs and to jazz up the oils.

Flavoured oils shouldn't be confined to salads. Use in marinades, trickle over grilled meats or

fish – or pour into a dish and serve as a dip with a selection of freshly baked breads.

Herb butters add a lovely finishing touch to cooked fish or chicken and are easy to make. Simply beat your favourite herb into some softened butter, perhaps adding a little pepper or lemon juice. Wrap in clingfilm and chill until required.

fennel and lemon butter

The flavour of fennel goes very well with fish. For a particularly satisfying result, melt a tablespoon of the butter into a piece of fried salmon fillet.

125 g lightly salted butter, softened
2 tablespoons chopped fennel fronds
grated zest of half a lemon
a little freshly ground black pepper

Makes about 125 g

Put the butter, fennel, lemon zest and pepper in a bowl and beat them until the butter is evenly speckled green. Pat it into a roll, wrap in clingfilm and chill until needed.

coriander and spring onion butter

The pungency of coriander and the sweetness of spring onion combine to make a butter that can give a new meaning to mashed potatoes.

125 g lightly salted butter, softened
2 tablespoons chopped coriander
1 spring onion, finely chopped

Makes about 125 g

Follow the method given for fennel and lemon butter, but replace the fronds of fennel with the coriander and spring onion. Chill until required. Beat into hot mashed potatoes.

pepper and chive butter

Roasted cod fillets taste even better when topped with this mildly onion-flavoured butter.

125 g lightly salted butter, softened
2 tablespoons chopped chives
1 tablespoon mixed peppercorns, lightly crushed

Makes about 125 g

Follow the method given for fennel and lemon butter, but replace the fronds of fennel with the chives and peppercorns. Chill until required. Serve with roasted fillets of cod or other white fish.

snacks and starters

ricotta baked with fresh herbs and chilli

This is an easy way to cook ricotta that makes an ideal light lunch. Small rounds of ricotta are available from most Italian delis – or you can use wedges cut from a larger cheese.

450 g whole ricotta
2 garlic cloves, sliced
1 red chilli, deseeded and sliced
½ teaspoon lightly crushed coriander seeds
4 tablespoons extra virgin olive oil
4 fresh bay leaves, lightly crushed
1 tablespoon freshly grated Parmesan cheese,
*   plus extra to serve*
sea salt and freshly ground black pepper
basil oil (page 90) or salsa verde (page 96)
*   and toasted bread, to serve*

Serves 4–6

Put the whole ricotta in a foil-lined baking dish. Put the garlic, chilli, coriander seeds and oil in a bowl and mix. Trickle the oil mixture over the cheese and tuck the bay leaves underneath.

Sprinkle Parmesan, salt and pepper over the ricotta and bake in a preheated oven at 190°C (375°F) Gas 5 for 20 minutes, basting halfway through.

Serve the ricotta spread onto some toasted bread trickled with basil oil or salsa verde. Finish with a sprinkling of grated Parmesan.

Herb-based sauces or spreads can be served as dips for crudités or spooned onto grilled fish or poultry. Zhatar is a Middle Eastern street snack traditionally sold rolled up in a cone of paper with hard-boiled eggs.

salsa verde

25 g parsley leaves
15 g mixed herbs, such as basil,
chives, coriander and mint
1 garlic clove, chopped
15 g green olives, pitted
1 tablespoon capers, rinsed and drained
2 anchovy fillets, rinsed and chopped
1 teaspoon Dijon mustard
2 teaspoons lemon juice
125 ml extra virgin olive oil
sea salt and freshly ground black pepper
vegetables and bread, to serve

Serves 6

Put all the ingredients except the oil in a food processor and blend to form a smooth paste. Gradually blend in the oil to form a sauce, then add salt and pepper to taste.

Serve as a dip with a selection of raw or cooked vegetables and fresh bread.

zhatar

15 g thyme leaves
1½ tablespoons sesame seeds, toasted
¼ teaspoon sea salt

Serves 4

Put the ingredients in a blender and work to a fine powder. Serve with hard-boiled eggs.

zhug

25 g coriander leaves
2–4 garlic cloves
1 teaspoon caraway seeds
1 teaspoon cumin seeds
seeds from 3 cardamom pods
1 large red chilli, deseeded and diced
2 tablespoons extra virgin olive oil
sea salt and freshly ground black pepper

Serves 4

Put all the ingredients in a food processor and blend until smooth. Add salt and pepper to taste and serve with char-grilled pita or lavash bread.

little pizzas with herb oil

This is a variation on hot garlic bread, in which small, thin pizza bases are doused in rosemary, garlic and pepper oil.

250 g strong plain flour
1 teaspoon easy-blend dried
* yeast*
1 teaspoon sea salt
1 tablespoon extra virgin
* olive oil (or a flavoured oil)*

herb topping
2 large garlic cloves, sliced
leaves from 4 sprigs of
* rosemary*
rosemary, garlic and pepper
* oil (see page 90)*

Makes 4 small or 2 large pizzas

Sift the flour into a food-mixer bowl and stir in the yeast and salt. With the dough hook turning, slowly pour in the oil and enough hot water, about 120 ml, to form a slightly sticky dough. Knead for 10 minutes.

Shape the dough into a ball. Put it in an oiled bowl, cover with clingfilm, and let rise for about 1 hour until the ball has doubled in size. Preheat the oven to 230°C (450°F) Gas 8 and put a pizza stone or baking sheet on the top shelf to heat.

Knock back the dough and divide it into 2 or 4 pieces. Put 1 piece on a floured surface and roll it out to form a thin round base. Mix the rosemary leaves and garlic with 6–8 tablespoons rosemary, garlic and pepper oil and sprinkle a little of the mixture over the pizza base.

Transfer the base to the preheated pizza stone or baking sheet and bake for 10–12 minutes until puffed and golden. Sprinkle a little extra rosemary, garlic and pepper oil over it. Continue to roll out and cook the pizzas one at a time, eating them as they come out of the oven.

Vietnamese herb and prawn rolls

Rice noodles, prawns and fragrant herbs are rolled up in rice paper wrappers and served with *nuóc cham* – a traditional Vietnamese dipping sauce.

Start by making the *nuóc cham*. Put the fish sauce, sugar, chilli and lime juice in a bowl. Add 2 tablespoons of water and leave to infuse for 1 hour.

Cook the noodles in a large saucepan of lightly salted boiling water for 3 minutes. Drain and refresh in cold water. Drain again, then mix with 1 tablespoon of the dipping sauce.

To rehydrate the rice paper wrappers, dip them one by one into a bowl of cold water for a few seconds until softened. Lay each wrapper flat and top with a small handful of cooked noodles, 2 or 3 prawns, a few pea shoots or bean sprouts and a few herb leaves.

Fold over the ends of the wrappers and roll them up to enclose the filling. Serve with the dipping sauce.

nuóc cham
3 tablespoons fish sauce
2 tablespoons caster sugar
1 large red chilli, deseeded and finely chopped
juice of ½ lime

1 bundle (60g) beanthread or vermicelli rice noodles
12 small rice paper wrappers (available from Chinese supermarkets)
24–36 large cooked prawns, peeled
50 g pea shoots or bean sprouts
12 Thai basil leaves (optional)
12 mint leaves
12 coriander leaves

Serves 6

main courses

sea bass with fragrant Thai oil

For this dish you need either 2 woks or 2 large bamboo steamers. The easiest way to cook the fish is to lay them on large pieces of foil and put these on the racks of the woks or in the bottom of the steamers, so that all the delicious juices settle in the foil.

Wash and dry the sea bass inside and out, and slash each side diagonally several times with a sharp knife. Put 2 fish on each of 2 large sheets of foil.

Mix the ginger, onion and garlic in a bowl. Put some of the mixture into each cavity, add a few slices of lime and a couple of coriander sprigs, then sprinkle the rest over the fish.

Mix the tamari, mirin and 2 tablespoons of the Thai oil together in a jug or bowl, then trickle the mixture over the fish. Put the foil parcels on racks set in 2 separate woks or into the base of 2 steamers. Cover tightly with lids and steam for 12 minutes. Remove from the heat, but leave undisturbed for a further 5 minutes.

Sprinkle the fish with chopped coriander and serve it with the juices, steamed rice and steamed Chinese greens.

4 sea bass, 500 g each, gutted
*   *and scaled*
5 cm fresh ginger, peeled and
*   *sliced*
4 spring onions, finely chopped
2 garlic cloves, sliced
1 lime, sliced
4 large sprigs of coriander
4 tablespoons tamari
*   *(Japanese soy sauce)*
2 tablespoons mirin (sweetened
*   *Japanese rice wine)*
6 tablespoons fragrant Thai oil
*   *(see page 90)*
chopped coriander leaves,
*   *steamed rice, and Chinese*
*   *greens, to serve*

Serves 4

red mullet saltimbocca with orange and sage

The Italian saltimbocca of veal escalope topped with Parma ham and sage inspired this dish. Red mullet is a rich fish, able to take the strong flavours of both ham and herb. The sweet/sharp sauce of orange and capers is the perfect foil.

2 oranges
8 large red mullet fillets, scaled
freshly ground black pepper
8 slices Parma ham
16 large sage leaves
3 tablespoons extra virgin olive oil
25 g lightly salted butter
2 tablespoons capers, rinsed and drained
75 ml white wine

Serves 4

Peel and segment one of the oranges, reserving the juices in a bowl. Squeeze the juice of the other orange into the bowl.

Wash and dry the mullet fillets and season them with pepper. Lay the Parma ham slices flat and top each with a fish fillet and a sage leaf. Drizzle a little oil over the top. Starting from one narrow end, carefully roll up each piece of ham, enclosing the fillet, and secure it with a cocktail stick.

Heat the remaining oil and the butter together in an ovenproof frying pan. Add the rolls of mullet and quickly brown them on all sides. Add the capers, wine, orange juice and remaining sage leaves to the pan. Cover with a layer of foil and bake in a preheated oven at 200°C (400°F) Gas 6 for 8 minutes. Remove the pan from the oven, transfer the rolls to a warm plate and let rest for 5 minutes.

Meanwhile, add the orange segments to the pan and heat through on top of the stove. Serve the saltimbocca with the sauce, a green salad and some bread to mop up the delicious juices.

chilli beef with avocado and coriander salsa

The chilli-marinated steaks can be grilled or cooked on a barbecue. The heat of the chilli sauce is tempered by the coolness of the avocado and the crème fraîche. For a fabulous picnic sandwich, let the steaks cool, then slice them and stuff each into a pita pocket with a spoonful of the salsa and another of crème fraîche or sour cream.

4 fillet steaks, about 200 g each
2 tablespoons hot chilli sauce or harissa paste
2 tablespoons olive oil
4 tablespoons crème fraîche or sour cream
sprigs of coriander, to serve

avocado and coriander salsa
1 large ripe Hass avocado
2 ripe tomatoes, skinned, deseeded and diced
freshly squeezed juice of ½–1 lime
1 garlic clove, crushed
1 small red chilli, deseeded and diced
2 tablespoons chopped coriander
1 tablespoon extra virgin olive oil
sea salt and freshly ground black pepper

Serves 4

Put the steaks in a shallow dish and rub them all over with the chilli sauce and oil. Marinate at room temperature for 1–4 hours.

Just before cooking, cut the avocado in half and take out the stone. Using a teaspoon, scoop the flesh into a bowl. Mix in the tomato, lime juice, garlic, chilli, coriander and oil, and season with salt and pepper.

Heat a stove-top grill pan for 3–4 minutes until very hot. Add the steaks and cook for 2 minutes each side, then let rest for 5 minutes.

Serve the steaks topped with the avocado and coriander salsa, the crème fraîche or sour cream, and sprigs of coriander.

1.75 kg free range chicken
25 g fresh curry leaves or 15 g dried
125 g lightly salted butter
1 lemon, halved
1 whole head of garlic,
    cloves separated
sea salt and freshly ground
    black pepper

Serves 4

butter-roasted chicken
with curry leaves

In some places, the leaves of the curry plant can be bought fresh or dried at Indian food stores. Where they are not available, you can substitute sprigs of tarragon.

Wash the chicken and pat dry with kitchen paper. Season the inside of the cavity with salt and pepper, and add a couple of sprigs of curry leaves. Cut several slashes in the flesh of each thigh. Finely chop (or tear) most of the remaining curry leaves and put them in a bowl, then beat in the butter with a wooden spoon.

Release the skin of the chicken from the flesh by inserting fingers under the skin at the neck end. Lift the skin away from the breast meat and slip half the butter mixture under it, smoothing it flat. Rub the rest all over the outside of the skin, pushing it well down into the slashes. Squeeze the juice of 1 lemon half over the chicken and put the other half into the cavity.

Arrange the garlic cloves and remaining curry leaves in a roasting tin. Put the chicken on top and roast in a preheated oven at 200°C (400°F) Gas 6 for about 1 hour 5 minutes. Pierce the thickest part of the thigh with a skewer, penetrating as far as the joint: if the juices run clear, the chicken is cooked. Let it rest for 5 minutes before carving.

spring herb risotto

The flavours of the herbs blend with the creaminess of the rice and cheese in this light, fragrant risotto. It is particularly good topped with a seared fillet of salmon or pan-fried cod.

50 g baby spinach leaves, shredded
50 g chopped mixed herbs, such as chervil,
  chives, mint, parsley and tarragon
4 tablespoons extra virgin olive oil
1 onion, finely chopped
2 garlic cloves, crushed
2 small leeks, well washed,
  trimmed and sliced
300 g arborio rice
150 ml dry white wine
50 g mascarpone cheese
50 g freshly grated Parmesan cheese, plus
  extra to serve
sea salt and freshly ground black pepper

Serves 4

Put 1.25 litres of water in a large saucepan and heat to a rolling boil. Add the spinach and herbs, return to the boil and immediately strain (reserving the liquid); refresh the spinach and herbs under cold water. Pat dry with kitchen paper and set aside.

Heat the oil in a deep frying pan. Add the onion, garlic and leeks and fry gently for 10 minutes. Add the rice and stir the mixture over the heat for 1 minute until all the grains are glossy. Pour in the wine and boil until almost totally evaporated.

In a separate saucepan, heat the reserved herb water until just simmering. Add the water to the rice, one ladle at a time, and simmer, stirring, until absorbed, before adding more. Repeat until all the water has been used and the rice is tender but still firm.

Stir in spinach, herbs, mascarpone and Parmesan. Cover and let stand for 5 minutes. Season with salt and pepper. Serve with extra Parmesan.

accompaniments

mixed leaf and herb salad with pine nut dressing

The pine nuts add a rich, creamy flavour and texture to this salad dressing, which perfectly complements the aromatic herbs and leaves. Mix a good selection of fresh herbs – basil, chervil, chives, dill, mint and parsley, for example – with salad leaves such as red chicory, mizuna, rocket, cos, pusse, frisée, ruby chard and mustard leaves.

500 g mixed leaves and 100 g mixed herbs

pine nut dressing
2 tablespoons pine nuts
4 tablespoons extra virgin olive oil
2 teaspoons sherry vinegar
sea salt and freshly ground pepper

Serves 4

Put the salad leaves and herbs in a very large bowl.

To make the dressing, heat 2 tablespoons of oil in a frying pan, add the pine nuts and fry for 3–4 minutes until evenly golden. Let cool.

Using a mortar and pestle, smash the nuts until they are mushy. Stir in the remaining oil. Add the vinegar, and season to taste. Pour the dressing over the salad and toss well until all the leaves are coated. Serve at once.

charred leek salad with tarragon vinegar dressing

In this lovely 'smoky' salad the charred peppers and leeks are well set off by the sharpness of the tarragon-infused vinegar dressing, which must be made in advance.

2 small bell peppers
350 g baby leeks, well washed and trimmed
olive oil
125 g French beans, trimmed
125 g baby spinach leaves
50 g pitted black olives
1 quantity tarragon vinegar dressing (see page 89)
sea salt and freshly ground pepper
Parmesan shavings, to serve

Serves 4

Heat a large stove-top grill pan for 3 minutes. Add the whole peppers and cook for 10–15 minutes, turning occasionally, until well charred all over. Transfer to a bowl, cover with a clean tea towel and let cool.

Toss the leeks in a little oil. Add to the grill pan and cook over a low heat for 10–12 minutes until evenly charred. Let cool and cut in half crossways. At the same time, blanch the beans in a large saucepan of lightly salted boiling water for 3–4 minutes. Drain, refresh under cold water and pat dry.

Slip the skins off the peppers, cut them in half and remove all the seeds. Cut the flesh into strips and toss the strips with the charred leeks and the beans. Arrange on a large plate. Scatter the spinach leaves and olives over the salad and sprinkle with plenty of the salad dressing. Add the Parmesan shavings and serve at once.

smashed celeriac with horseradish

The grated horseradish makes this deliciously rich 'smash' a good partner for roast beef – or substitute chopped mint for the parsley and serve with a grilled lamb chop.

4 tablespoons extra virgin olive oil, plus extra to mash
2 garlic cloves, crushed
6 spring onions, trimmed and chopped
500 g celeriac, peeled and finely diced
500 g potatoes, peeled and finely diced
75 g horseradish, peeled and finely grated
  (or 3 tablespoons ready-grated)
300 ml vegetable stock
2 tablespoons chopped parsley
sea salt and freshly ground black pepper

Serves 4

Heat the oil in a saucepan, add the garlic and onion and fry gently for 5 minutes. Remove with a slotted spoon and set aside. Add the celeriac, potatoes and horseradish to the pan and fry for a further 5 minutes.

Pour in the stock, bring to the boil, cover and simmer gently for 25–30 minutes until the vegetables are tender. Remove lid and boil until the liquid is reduced to the point where almost nothing remains and the mixture is sticky.

Stir in the reserved garlic and onion. Add the parsley, salt and pepper and mash coarsely, beating in more olive oil to taste.

slow-roasted tomato salad with opal basil

This pretty salad can be served either as an accompaniment or as a light lunch or starter. When opal basil leaves are not available, ordinary green basil can be used instead.

6 ripe tomatoes, halved
1 tablespoon olive oil
2 balls buffalo mozzarella cheese
a few sprigs of opal basil
1 quantity basil oil (see page 90)
balsamic vinegar
mizuna leaves
sea salt and freshly ground black pepper

Serves 4

Put the halved tomatoes in a small roasting tin so that they fit in a single layer. Sprinkle with the olive oil, season liberally with salt and pepper and roast in a preheated oven at 150°C (300°F) Gas 2 for 3 hours until shrunken and glossy. Let cool.

Just before serving, tear the mozzarella into small pieces and arrange on a large plate. Add the tomato halves, then sprinkle the opal basil leaves over the tomatoes and cheese and trickle a generous amount of the basil oil and a little vinegar over the salad.

Season to taste with salt and pepper, and serve the salad topped with mizuna leaves.

sweet things

apricots poached in tarragon syrup

A delicately flavoured tarragon and vanilla syrup perfumes the fresh apricots as they cook and then cool. The poached fruits can be enjoyed at their best when served with home-made vanilla ice cream or Greek yoghurt.

125 g caster sugar
2 pieces lemon zest, cut into thin strips
1 vanilla pod, split lengthways
6 large sprigs of tarragon, lightly crushed
12 apricots, halved and pitted
1 tablespoon tarragon vinegar (see page 89)
  or lemon juice
vanilla ice cream or Greek yoghurt, to serve

Serves 6

Put the sugar and 300 ml water in a wide saucepan and heat gently to dissolve the sugar. Add the strips of lemon zest, the vanilla pod and the tarragon sprigs. Bring to the boil.

Add the apricots and simmer gently for about 5 minutes until softened. Remove the pan from the heat. Stir in the tarragon vinegar or lemon juice and let cool.

Serve with ice cream or yoghurt.

strawberry, melon and basil salad

This fragrant concoction is best served slightly chilled. The pairing of basil and strawberries is surprisingly good, but other herbs such as fresh mint, lemon verbena and lemon balm can work equally well.

1 cantaloupe melon, halved, deseeded, sliced and peeled
250 g strawberries, hulled and halved
180 ml Muscat de Beaumes de Venise or other dessert wine
a few basil leaves

Serves 4

Put the slices of melon in a large bowl with the strawberries. Pour the wine over the fruit and chill for 30 minutes. Top with the basil leaves and serve.

lemon and rosemary posset with raspberries

Rosemary goes very well with lemon and is excellent in creamy puddings. The refreshing flavour and simplicity of this dish make it ideal for dinner parties. The posset should be prepared in advance and chilled overnight in ramekin dishes.

600 ml double cream
4 large sprigs of rosemary, washed and bruised
100 g caster sugar
100 ml freshly squeezed lemon juice
125 g raspberries
1 tablespoon framboise or crème de cassis

Serves 6

Put the cream and rosemary sprigs in a saucepan and heat gently to boiling point. Remove from the heat and leave to infuse for 20 minutes. Discard the rosemary.

Add the sugar to the cream and return to the boil. Simmer for 3 minutes. Stir in the lemon juice, then immediately pour the mixture into six ramekins. Chill overnight.

Marinate the raspberries in framboise or crème de cassis for 30 minutes. Spoon the fruit onto the creams and serve.

mint chocolate chip ice cream

Heating mint with milk and cream gives a wonderfully fresh flavour to this ice cream, which is a million miles away from the bright-green synthetically flavoured version that is available commercially.

500 ml full-cream milk
300 ml double cream
4 large sprigs of mint
5 egg yolks
125 g caster sugar
75 g dark chocolate, cut into small dice

Serves 8

Put the milk, cream and mint sprigs in a saucepan and heat gently to boiling point. Remove from the heat and leave to infuse for 20 minutes, then return to boiling point.

Meanwhile beat the egg yolks and sugar in a bowl. Stir in the hot milk mixture, and return it to the pan. Stir the custard over a low heat until it thickens to coat the back of a wooden spoon. Do not let the mixture boil or it will curdle. Strain into a clean bowl and leave until cold.

Freeze in an ice cream maker according to manufacturer's instructions – or freeze in a plastic container, beating at hourly intervals until creamy and frozen. Add the chocolate chips just before the mixture freezes. Serve immediately or freeze until required.

herbal coolers

iced long island tea with lemon verbena

4 tea bags (Indian tea is best)
a bunch of lemon verbena
2 limes, sliced
ice cubes
lemonade

Serves 4

Place the tea bags in a jug and add 1 litre cold water. Chill for 1 hour, then discard the tea bags.

Put the lemon verbena, slices of lime and plenty of ice cubes in a large clean jug. Add the tea and top up with lemonade. Serve cold.

apple and lemon grass cordial

1 litre organic apple juice (unsweetened)
250 g caster sugar
4 large stalks lemon grass,
*   halved lengthways*
lemon wedges, ice cubes, mineral water
*   and lemon grass stalks, to serve*

Makes about 750 ml

Put the apple juice and sugar in a saucepan and heat until the sugar dissolves. Add the lemon grass and simmer for 10 minutes. Let cool, then strain into a clean bottle.

To dilute, pour a little syrup into tall glasses. Add ice cubes and lemon, and top up with still or sparkling mineral water. Add a stalk of lemon grass to each glass and stir well.

melon and mint frappé

2 large ripe melons
15 g mint leaves
freshly squeezed juice of 2 limes
a little honey (optional)
ice cubes, to serve

Serves 4

Halve, deseed, slice and peel the melon and put the flesh in a blender. Add the mint leaves, lime juice and honey, if using, and blend until smooth. Serve with ice cubes.

A–Z of herbs

A selection of herbs that flavour food or provide garden ornament.

(Heights given are the maximum heights to which plants can grow in optimum conditions.)

Agastache foeniculum
Anise hyssop

Aromatic, hardy, short-lived perennial that grows to 60 cm (2 ft) in flower. Heart-shaped leaves with scalloped edges. Purple or whitish flower spikes in summer. Sow seed in pots in heated propagator in spring. Grows in full sun in average soil, but does best in moist loam. Add dried flower spikes and leaves to potpourri.

Allium fistulosum
Welsh onion

Hardy evergreen perennial, also known as Japanese onion or Japanese leek. Flowers from second year, and reaches 60–90 cm (2–3 ft). Growth similar to spring onion, but has larger stems. Overwinters in coldest conditions. Sow in fertile soil in sun in spring, or divide clumps. Harvest whole onions, or chop leaves as you would chives.

Allium sativum
Garlic

Hardy perennial grown as an annual. Reaches 40–60 cm (16–24 in). Narrow leaves similar to those of leeks. Plant in autumn in full sun; harvest as soon as leaves die down. Bulbs are delicious roasted; also used in marinades and salad dressings and to flavour meat. Wild garlic (*A. ursinum*) needs moist woodland conditions; leaves are added to salads and soups.

Allium schoenoprasum
Chives

Hardy perennial with fine green foliage and mauve or white pompom flowers. Depending on species or variety, grows to 30–40 cm (12–16 in) with a spread of 10–20 cm (4–8 in). Grow in full sun in moisture-retentive soil; divide congested clumps in spring or autumn. Flowers and leaves are used in salads, egg dishes and soups. Add to hot dishes at the last moment to prevent loss of flavour.

Allium tuberosum
Chinese chives, garlic chives

Hardy perennial that grows to 40 cm (16 in). Leaves are as long as ordinary chives but flattened and have a strong garlic aroma. Sow seed outside in late spring; divide clumps in spring. Good in salads and cooked dishes.

Aloe barbadensis
Aloe vera

Succulent half-hardy perennial with fleshy spike-edged leaves. Can grow to 60 cm (2 ft) in a large pot, but is usually much smaller. Sow seed in pots in propagator at 21°C (70°F); germination is erratic – do not lose hope if nothing happens in the first year. Propagate from offshoots in summer. Use loam-based compost with added grit. Water sparingly and repot in spring. Plants can be grown outside in summer but must be overwintered in a frost-free place, at a minimum of 5°C (40°F). The gel from its leaf soothes minor burns and cuts; also used in cosmetic preparations.

Aloysia triphylla
syn. *Lippia citriodora*
Lemon verbena

Half-hardy deciduous perennial. Grows to 3 m (10 ft) with a spread of 2.5 m (8 ft). Pale-green and lemon-scented lance-shaped leaves; terminal panicles of lilac-tinged white flowers. Likes full sun and free-draining light soil. If grown in garden against a sunny wall, needs frost protection. A good deep mulch will keep plant safe in milder climates; in colder areas pot it up and overwinter in frost-free greenhouse. Grow from seed or softwood cuttings in spring. Take cuttings from ripened wood in late summer. A relaxing tisane can be made from the leaves; also used to scent vinegars; dried, it is added to potpourri or herb pillows.

Anethum graveolens
Dill

Annual varying in height from 60 cm (2 ft) to 150 cm (5 ft). Some varieties are suited to leaf or seed production. Dill needs well-drained gritty soil and full sun. Sow seed in rows as soon as soil warms up in spring. Thin to about 20 cm (8 in) apart to make sturdy plants. Water in the mornings; plants will run to seed if kept too dry. Sow in succession for a good kitchen supply.

Angelica archangelica
Angelica

Biennial or short-lived perennial that dies after flowering. Grows up to 2.5 m (8 ft), but usually 1–1.5 m (3–5 ft). A good ornamental plant in a herb border in part-shade. Self-seeds copiously. Cooking angelica with rhubarb reduces the need for added sugar; stems can be candied. Should be used medicinally only on medical advice and never by diabetes sufferers.

Anthriscus cerefolium
Chervil

Hardy annual that reaches 30–60 cm (1–2 ft) in flower. Sow seed in light soil. Part shade is best for production of abundant leaves. In a hot dry climate goes to seed prematurely. A component of the traditional *fines herbes* bundle.

Armoracia rusticana
Horseradish

Hardy perennial. Grows to 60–90 cm (24–36 in). *A. r.* 'Variegata' has prettily marked leaves in cream and green and makes a fine centrepiece in a herb garden (though the flavour is not as good or strong for culinary use as that of the non-variegated type).

Cichorium intybus Chicory

Coriandrum sativum Coriander

Helichrysum italicum Curry plant

Artemisia dracunculus
Tarragon

French tarragon grows to 90 cm (3 ft); Russian tarragon, *A. dracunculoides*, is slightly taller, reaching 1.2 m (4 ft). Both have a spread of 45 cm (18 in). Grow in a dry sunny site with winter protection. Propagate French tarragon from root cuttings; it is not as hardy as the Russian variety and has no viable seed. Tarragon is good with chicken and fish; French tarragon has much the better flavour.

Atriplex hortensis
Orach

Annual grown as a culinary and an ornamental herb. Grows to 1.5 m (4 ft) or more, with a spread of 30 cm (12 in); can grow higher, depending on the quality of the soil. Seed heads are used in cut-flower arrangements in some countries. Use tender young leaves in cooking: a popular spinach substitute in Europe.

Barbarea verna
Landcress

Hardy biennial that grows to 20–70 cm (8–28 in) with a spread of 20 cm (8 in). Sow in rich moist soil, in summer for winter use and in spring for summer use. Prefers sun but will grow in all but deepest shade. Peppery flavour of leaves makes them a good watercress substitute in salads; use before plant flowers.

Borago officinalis
Borage

Hardy annual that grows to about 60 cm (24 in); sometimes plants overwinter and grow into a second season. Bristly branches, and leaves with a strong cucumber-like smell; blue or white star-like flowers. Sow seed in spring. Grow in light soil in a sunny position. Edible flowers can be crystallized for decorative use or added fresh to fruit cups. Borage may cause contact dermatitis.

Buxus sempervirens
Box

Hardy to half-hardy evergreen used extensively as an edging plant in herb gardens. Grows from 1 m (3 ft) to 5 m (15 ft), and higher in old unclipped specimens. Leaves are neatly egg-shaped to elliptical, often glossy dark to mid-green, and some cultivars are variegated. Box grows in sun or shade; prefers alkaline soil but, as long as the ground is not waterlogged, is not too fussy. If a hedge is planted, prepare the soil well with compost and well-rotted manure. Take cuttings in spring or summer. Box has no culinary use and all parts are poisonous. It has traditional medical uses.

Calendula officinalis
Pot marigold

Hardy annual, but some plants will overwinter successfully. Grows to 60 cm (24 in). Daisy-like flowers, single or double, vary in colour from pale cream to deep orange. Whole plant is aromatic. Marigold grows in most soils in full sun. Sow seed in spring or autumn. Self-sown seedlings are capable of overwintering in sheltered outside positions, but don't rely on this. Deadhead plants regularly to extend flowering season. Culinary and medicinal plant; also used in cosmetic preparations. Dried petals look good in potpourris.

Chamaemelum nobile
Chamomile

Height varies from 6 cm (2.5 in) to 60 cm (24 in) depending on species or cultivar. Non-flowering 'Treneague' – the chamomile commonly used for chamomile lawns – is increased by division and the taking of cuttings, as is the double-flowered chamomile. For others, sow seed in pots or straight into the ground; use bottom heat for pots in spring and sow in ground when it has warmed up. Grow in free-draining soil in full sun. Main uses are cosmetic and medicinal.

Chenopodium bonus-henricus
Good King Henry

Perennial that can reach 60 cm (24 in) with a spread of 45 cm (18 in). Sow seed in fertile soil in spring in a sunny position. Thin out to 25 cm (10 in) apart. Leaves used as a spinach substitute. Seeds are mildly laxative; do not use if you suffer from kidney problems or rheumatism.

Cichorium intybus
Chicory

Hardy perennial reaching a height in flower of 1 m (3 ft). Leaves are long, blunt and spear-shaped, with coarsely toothed edges. Blue flowers from summer to autumn. Sow seed in spring in open sunny situation; prefers alkaline soil but will grow almost anywhere. Leaves are added to salads.

Coriandrum sativum
Coriander

Tender annual growing to 60–70 cm (24–28 in) with a spread of about 30 cm (12 in). *C.s.* 'Cilantro' is best for leaf production and *C.s.* 'Morocco' for seed. Sow seed in spring in a light well-drained soil when threat of frost is past and soil has warmed up. Thin seedlings as they grow and keep watered for leaf production, but do not overwater. Seeds and leaves are used in cooking and medicinally.

Cryptotaenia japonica
Japanese parsley, mitsuba

Hardy perennial that grows to 30 cm (12 in) before flowering and 60–90 cm (2–3 ft) in flower. Leaf is like celery; white flowers dotted about in small umbels. Likes moist conditions in part shade. Grows in sun or in the shade of larger plants in moisture-retentive soil. Leaves and stems used in cooking.

Curcuma longa
Turmeric

Perennial tropical herb of the ginger family. Can be grown as a container plant in temperate climates, but needs winter protection. Grow in a peat and loam mixture, with added grit or sharp sand. Likes warm moist air conditions. Do not overwater. Root is dried and ground into powder for culinary and medicinal uses.

Cymbopogon citratus
Lemon grass

Perennial tropical grass with a strong lemon scent that reaches 60–90 cm (2–3 ft) in the greenhouse. Grow in pots from offshoots or seed. Use peat and loam mixture, with added grit or sharp sand to ensure good drainage. Do not overwater. Likes consistently warm conditions; reduce watering or do not water at all if it is overcast or raining for any length of time. Used in Indian and Thai cookery.

Dianthus species
Pinks

Height varies from 15 cm (8 in) to 60 cm (24 in), depending on species. Grow from softwood cuttings in spring or heel cuttings in late summer. Some older cultivars have to be propagated directly after flowering; they may also be divided then. Grow in full sun in well-drained poor soil; most pinks also make good rock-garden plants. Petals have culinary and medicinal uses; dried petals are included in scented sachets.

Echinacea purpurea
Echinacea, purple coneflower

Hardy perennial that grows to 1.2 m (4 ft). Sow seed in early spring in a plug tray in greenhouse or propagator, or divide existing plants (in autumn or spring) and plant in border or herb garden. Grow in well-drained soil that will retain a bit of moisture in full sun. Echinacea seems to boost the immune system, thereby helping the body to fight infection, and is used extensively in the pharmaceutical industry. There are several good ornamental cultivars.

Eruca versicaria
Rocket

Half-hardy annual with a height of 60–90 cm (2–3 ft) in flower. Leaves are oval or lance-shaped; flowers are whitish with darker veining. Sow seed from spring onwards in partial shade in moisture-retentive soil. Sow in autumn for winter salads. Cover with a cloche in severe weather. Hard frost and snow will kill rocket, but in mild areas it can be harvested for most of the winter. Adds peppery vigour to salads and cold dishes.

Eucalyptus citriodora
Eucalyptus

Tender evergreen tree. Can grow to more than 30 m (100 ft) in its native habitat. A good scented conservatory plant that can be taken outside to a sheltered patio. Sow seed in winter or spring. If kept in pots, feed during growing season. Used in cosmetics and pharmaceuticals.

Foeniculum vulgare
Fennel

Growing to 2.1 m (7 ft) in height, with a spread of 45 cm (18 in), this short-lived perennial is best sown straight into a permanent site. Cultivated for its culinary and medicinal purposes, fennel, especially the bronze form, is also a useful ornamental; its yellow flowers are carried in umbels in summer.

Fragaria vesca
Wild strawberry

Hardy perennial that grows to 15–30 cm (6–12 in). Leaves are divided into heavily serrated leaflets. White-petalled flowers and sweet, scented fruit that may be red or white. Sow seed in late winter or early spring in pots in the greenhouse, or divide existing plants after fruiting. Grow in fertile moist soil in full sun or part shade.

Galium odoratum
syn. Asperula odorata
Sweet woodruff

Hardy perennial. Grows to 20 cm (8 in) in flower and has an indefinite spread. Whole plant is aromatic. Leaves are mid-green in whorls. Star-shaped white blooms appear in late spring

or early summer. A plant for deep shade. Sow seed or propagate from root cuttings at almost any time, but the best time is after flowering; cut back and take small pieces of root to plant in pots or cuttings bed in part shade; water after planting. It will soon reshoot. Grows best in alkaline soil under deciduous shrubs and trees. Woodruff jelly is a delicacy in some parts of Europe.

Helichrysum italicum
Curry plant

Hardy evergreen perennial that grows to 60 cm (24 in) with a spread of up to 1 m (3 ft). Leaves are narrow and silver-felted; yellow button flowers appear in summer. The whole plant has a strong curry scent. Not much used in the kitchen, rather as an ornamental in gardens. Increase by cuttings in spring or autumn. Plant in well-drained soil in full sun. Prolonged wet combined with cold can kill the plant, so, in parts of the country where winters are cold and wet, grow in a large container or overwinter in a cold greenhouse.

Humulus lupulus
Hops

Hardy perennial herbaceous climber. Grows to 6 m (20 ft). Has male and female flowers on separate plants. Young leaves are heart-shaped; older leaves have three to five lobes. Whole plant is covered with tiny hooks. Sow in autumn in pots and overwinter in a cold frame. Take cuttings or divide female plants in spring or early summer. The golden form of hop is a showy ornamental and can be used in the same way as green hops.

Hyssopus officinalis
Hyssop

Hardy semi-evergreen perennial that grows to 80 cm (32 in) in flower. Leaves are narrow and aromatic; flowers are blue, pink or white depending on variety. Rock hyssop, *H.o.* ssp. *aristatus*, is a good rock-garden or pot plant with dark-blue flowers. Grow in well-drained average soil in full sun. In pots it may need a feed boost if grown in the same soil for several years. Sow seed in plug trays in heated propagator in spring. Cuttings can be taken in late spring and early summer from non-flowering shoots. Seed can also be sown straight into the ground. Thin out if grown as a hedge. Culinary and medicinal plant; use medicinally only on expert advice.

Juniperus communis
Juniper

Slow-growing hardy evergreen shrub or tree that grows to 4 m (25 ft). Needle-like narrow leaves with sharp-pointed tips. Whole plant is aromatic. Sow seed in autumn in pots and overwinter in cold frame or cold greenhouse. Take cuttings in spring or autumn. Do not use juniper berries in pregnancy or if you suffer from kidney problems.

Laurus nobilis
Bay

Tree or small shrub that grows to 8 m (26 ft), with a spread of 3 m (20 ft) or more. Buy as a well-grown ornamental and use surplus leaves for *bouquet garni* or to flavour oil or vinegar. Pick leaves straight from tree or keep a few dried in a covered jar.

Lavandula species
Lavender

Hardy or half-hardy evergreen perennials. Vary in height, according to species or cultivar, from 30 cm (12 in) to 90 cm (36 in). One of the most popular plants in the modern garden. All species like an open sunny position in fertile well-drained soil. Seed can be sown in autumn or spring in propagator; overwinter autumn-sown seed in cold greenhouse. Seed, except that from *L. stoechas*, is variable. Cut back plants after flowering, and for a neat bush trim again in spring. Leaves are all very narrow; flower spikes are usually mauve/purple, pale blue or dark blue. Culinary and medicinal herb that is also used in distilled form in cosmetics.

Levisticum officinale
Lovage

Hardy perennial. Grows to 2 m (6 ft) with a spread of up to 1 m (3 ft) or more. Grow in rich, moist, well-drained soil in full sun or part shade; sow seed in autumn outside, or in spring in pots in a propagator. Use young leaves in soups and salads; the flavour is better before flowering. Do not take during pregnancy or if you have kidney problems.

Lonicera species
Honeysuckle

L. periclymenum is a deciduous perennial that grows up to 7 m (23 ft). Its fragrant flowers with a pink/red blush are followed by (poisonous) red berries. *L. japonica* is a semi-evergreen deciduous perennial with a height of up to 10 m (30 ft); pale cream flowers turn yellow with age and are followed by black berries (also poisonous). Sow seed in autumn in pots to overwinter outside or in cold frame. Take cuttings in summer or layer at any time. Will grow in sun or part shade in most soils.

Malva sylvestris
Mallow

Biennial or short-lived perennial that, depending on variety, grows to 1.5 m (5 ft). Rounded leaves on basal rosette resemble those of *Alchemilla mollis*, and those that grow up the stem are finely cut or ivy-shaped. Mallows will tolerate most soils, but in overly moist may need staking. Fertile soil in sun or part shade will suit the plants best. Sow seed in autumn and overwinter in cold frame, or sow in spring in cool greenhouse. Seed can also be sown in the garden where the plants are to flower. Used in cooking.

Melissa officinalis
Lemon balm

Hardy perennial that grows to 80 cm (32 in). The golden form, *M. o.* 'All Gold', may need some protection in winter, so mulch with bracken or other foliage and keep this in place with a cloche. Keep 'All Gold' out of full sun or it will scorch. Golden and variegated forms are fine ornamentals; all are good bee plants. Increase by cuttings or division in autumn or spring. Loses its lemon fragrance when cooked, so use fresh in the kitchen.

Mentha
Mint

Grows to various heights depending on species; some are prostrate. Mint has spreading root runners and can be very invasive. The leaves of different species have different aromatic qualities. Most mints grow best in part or full shade and need to be restrained to prevent them from taking over whole beds. Cut back in midsummer to rejuvenate plants. Culinary and medicinal herb. Mint oil may cause an allergic reaction and must not be used on babies.

Monarda didyma
Bergamot, oswego tea, bee balm

Hardy perennial that, depending on species or cultivar, grows to between 75 cm (30 in) and 90 cm (36 ft), with a spread of 45 cm (18 in). Leaves are elliptical, sometimes toothed, with pointed tips. Flowers are in whorls; colours include pale purple, red, white, soft pink and purple. All cultivars have to be increased by division or cuttings. Seed from species should be sown in propagators. Grow in part shade in moist rich soil; in moisture-retentive soil it will grow in full sun. Mostly grown in herbaceous borders for its flowers, but also has culinary and medicinal uses.

Myrrhis odorata
Sweet Cicely

Hardy perennial that grows to between 60 cm (2 ft) and 90 cm (3 ft) in flower. Leaves are fern-like; small white flowers in large umbels. Sow seed in pots and overwinter in a cold frame because seeds need stratifying. Root cuttings can be taken in spring or autumn, and plants can be divided in spring. For best results, grow in well-drained poor soil. Cut back flower heads before they set seed.

Hyssopus officinalis Hyssop

Monarda didyma Bergamot

Oenothera biennis Evening primrose

Myrtus communis
Myrtle

Half-hardy evergreen shrub that grows to 3 m (10 ft). All parts are aromatic. In areas with cold wet winters and prolonged ground and air frosts, grow in pots and overwinter in frost-free greenhouse or conservatory. In milder areas, simply protect from too much winter rain. Grow in well-drained soil in full sun. If grown in pots, add grit and bark to loam-based compost. Take soft wood cuttings in spring and semi-ripe cuttings in late summer.

Ocimum basilicum
Basil

In temperate northern Europe basil is usually pot-grown, reaching 45 cm (18 in) with a spread of up to 30 cm (12 in). In Mediterranean regions it grows to twice the size or more, in the ground. Sow seed in spring either direct into the ground after frost, or into containers placed in a warm greenhouse or propagator. Transplant as soon as the plant is large enough to handle. Take care not to overwater. Wonderful in salads, in pesto sauce and with pasta.

Oenothera biennis
Evening primrose

Hardy biennial that can reach 1.2 m (4 ft). Lance-shaped leaves make a rosette in the first year, and in the second year the flower spike rises with large yellow, evening-scented flowers. Sow seed in spring in plug trays or in the place where you want it to grow. Grow in well-drained soil in a sunny position. Self-sows abundantly. Mainly medicinal, but all parts are edible and can be steamed and eaten.

Origanum vulgare
Oregano, marjoram

Several species and varieties; most are hardy in light soil and grow to a height and a spread of up to 60 cm (24 in). Species can be grown in spring in pots in propagator or in situ; soil should be free-draining and alkaline. Will not thrive in waterlogged soils. Best in full sun. Cultivars will not come true from seed and cuttings should be taken in late spring; plants can also be divided in spring. Used extensively in cooking. An infusion in the bath aids relaxation and a few drops of essential oil on the pillow promotes sleep.

Papaver somniferum
Opium poppy

Hardy annual. Grows to 90 cm (3 ft). Sow seed in autumn for early flowers and seeds, or in spring for later flowering, straight into the ground in a sunny, fertile, well-drained soil. Thin if necessary. Seeds used in baking and salads. Other parts used in pharmaceuticals.

Pelargonium species
Scented pelargoniums

Half-hardy evergreen shrubs that, depending on variety and species, grow to varying heights, from 30 cm to 1 m (12–40 in). Some species can be grown from seed but it is easier to grow them from cuttings, and all cultivars must be grown from cuttings. Take cuttings in summer or autumn as plants are being cut back prior to overwintering in a frost-free site. Grow in full sun in well-drained soil if in the ground; dig and pot up, reduce watering in autumn and keep watering to a minimum over winter.

Essential oils are used in aromatherapy. The scented leaves are sometimes used to flavour cakes and puddings but should be removed before serving.

Perilla frutescens
Perilla

Tender annual that makes a good ornamental in the flower border. Taller purple form can reach 90 cm (3 ft). Leaves slightly resemble a stinging nettle; can also be confused with the 'ruffles' type of basil. Start off in greenhouse or propagator. Transplant, and plant out once frosts are over. Grow in light well-drained soil in full sun or light shade. In cold areas grow in pots. Can stand cold a little better than basil, but likes similar treatment.

Petroselinum crispum
Parsley

Hardy biennial growing to 30 cm (12 in), and to 60 cm (24 in) in flower. Greenish-white flowers in second year. Various forms with heavily curled foliage; others with uncurled, flat leaves. All are good for salads and flavouring. Seeds are chewed in some countries as a remedy for bad breath. Also has a medicinal use but should be avoided during pregnancy.

Pimpinella anisum
Aniseed

Half-hardy annual. Grows to 45 cm (18 in) with a spread of 25 cm (10 in). Sow seed in light well-drained soil in a sunny position when frosts are over. Do not transplant; thin out to 20 cm (8 in) apart. Gather seeds on stalks in late summer just as they ripen, and dry off in paper bags. Seeds used in fruit dishes and Middle Eastern recipes.

Portulaca oleracea
Purslane

Half-hardy annual growing to 15 cm
(6 in) with a spread of 30 cm (12 in).
Green or golden leaves. Sow in plug
trays for early planting out or in rows
in full sun; thin out and use early in
season. Mild-flavoured leaves are good
in salads and complement stronger-
flavoured herbs and spices.

Primula vulgaris
Primrose

Spring-flowering perennial. Height and
spread of 15 cm (6 in). Club-shaped
leaves grow from basal rosette. Pale-
yellow flowers with delicate honey
scent grow singly from the rosette.
Grows in moist soil in sun or shade
and tolerates heavy soils. Start seed
off in pots in autumn. Leave outside in
cold frame or grow fresh seed straight
after harvest; germination can be
erratic. Plants can be divided in
autumn. Culinary and medicinal uses.

Rosa species
Rose

Old-fashioned roses, especially the
scented apothecary's rose, *R. gallica*
'Officinalis', were traditionally used in
herb gardens. Lax sprawling growth.
Scented petals are used in cosmetics,
to flavour food and in potpourri.

Rosmarinus officinalis
Rosemary

Numerous cultivars, some upright and
others prostrate. Prostrate group
reaches a height of 30 cm (12 in). The
largest rosemary has a height and a
spread of up to 2 m (6 ft). *R. officinalis*
can be grown from seed, but cultivars
need to be propagated from soft or

semi-ripe cuttings in spring or late
summer; they can also be layered.
Needs well-drained soil and a sunny
position. Grows well in containers.
Used in the kitchen, medicinally and
in cosmetic preparations, but avoid
during pregnancy. Essential oil must
not be taken internally.

Rumex acetosa
Sorrel

Sorrel and buckler leaf sorrel
(*R. scutatus*) are useful garden
plants. Buckler leaf sorrel grows to
15–45 cm (6–18 in) with a spread
of 12.5–60 cm (5–24 in). French
sorrel is a hardy perennial growing
to 60–120 cm (2–4 ft) with a spread
of 30 cm (1 ft). Sow seed in spring
in propagator from February onwards,
or in late spring outside. Can be
divided in spring or autumn. A good
culinary plant; also used in medicine
and, with alum as a mordant, makes
a yellow or green dye. Contains
oxalic acid, making it poisonous in
large doses. People with kidney
disease, rheumatism, gout or kidney
stones should avoid.

Salvia officinalis
Sage

Height and spread vary, depending on
species, up to 90 cm (3 ft) in height
and 70 cm (28 in) spread. Purple,
golden and tricoloured sages are good
ornamentals as well as culinary and
medicinal plants. Ideal container plant
for a sunny patio. Not all sages are
hardy. *S. elegans* (pineapple-scented
leaves) needs to be overwintered in
frost-free conditions. Grow from
cuttings in spring and summer and
replace plants every few years as they

become very woody. Grow in a light
free-draining soil in full sun. Dried
leaves can be added to potpourri.

Sambucus nigra
Elder

Deciduous hardy perennial shrub or
tree. Grows to 3–7 m (10–23 ft)
with a spread of up to 3.5 m (12 ft).
Good ornamental for borders or wild
hedgerows. Fruit must be cooked
if used in the kitchen. Flowers used
to make fritters and elderflower
champagne. Traditionally berries have
been made into a cordial for relieving
the symptoms of colds and coughs.

Sanguisorba minor
Salad burnet

Hardy evergreen perennial. Grows to
20–60 cm (8–24 in) with a spread of
30 cm (12 in). Sow seed in spring or
autumn; deadhead regularly. Culinary
and medicinal herb, much under-used
in the kitchen. Has a slight taste of
cucumber and goes well with fish,
cheese and salads, especially in winter,
when other herbs may be scarce.

Saponaria officinalis
Soapwort

Hardy perennial growing to 90 cm
(3 ft) or more. Tumbling lax plant with
lance-shaped oval leaves and clusters
of single flowers, but 'Rubra Plena'
has double flowers that are at first
pink and turn red with age. Can be
invasive. Sow seed in autumn, as soon
as ripe, in a cold frame. Plants appear
in spring. Germination is sometimes
erratic. Rootstock can be divided in
autumn or early spring. It has been
used medicinally, in cosmetics and
as an ingredient of soap.

***Rosa* 'Moonlight'** Rose

Saponaria officinalis Soapwort

Tropaeoleum majus Nasturtium

Satureja hortensis
Summer savory, bean herb

Half-hardy annual that in flower reaches 30 cm (12 in) with a spread of 20 cm (8 in). Grows bushier if growing tips are harvested often. Sow seed outside when frosts have finished, or sow in plug trays and transplant when soil has warmed up. Whole plant is aromatic. Use leaves before white or mauve flowers appear. Dries well, and is sold dried. In parts of Europe used in almost every dish that incorporates beans.

Satureja montana
Winter savory, mountain savory

Semi-evergreen hardy perennial that grows to 30 cm (12 in) with a spread of 30 cm (12 in) or more depending on conditions. Narrow, lance-shaped leaves; white flowers. Whole plant is very aromatic. Likes full sun and well-drained poor soil. Good ornamental in the right soil; suitable for rockeries. Take cuttings in spring, or sow seed in propagator or greenhouse in early spring. Seed needs light to germinate. In areas of high rainfall and heavy soil, overwinter some plants in pots, where watering can be minimized. Used to flavour soups, game and other meats.

Sesame indicum
Sesame

Annual tropical herb that grows to 60–90 cm (2–3 ft). Needs long hot summers to produce its nutty seeds. Collect seeds as they ripen before the capsules burst open. Sow after frost danger is past. In cool areas grow under cover. Start in pots in heated propagator to extend growing season. Leaves and seeds used in cooking.

Symphytum officinale
Comfrey

Hardy perennial growing to 1 m (3 ft). Lance-shaped bristly leaves; depending on species or cultivar, flowers can be cream, yellow, blue purple, pink or red. Sow seed in spring in garden; germination is erratic. Root cuttings or divisions produce plants more quickly. Grow in full sun or part shade; does best in deep moist soil. Used in organic gardening as liquid manure.

Tanacetum parthenium
Feverfew

Hardy short-lived perennial. Height varies from 60 cm (2 ft) to 120 cm (4 ft); sometimes smaller, especially golden feverfew, *T.p.* 'Aureum', which reaches 45 cm (18 in) in flower. Grow in rich soil in full sun. Deadhead often. Sow seed in spring or early autumn; overwinter plants from autumn sowing in cold frame or heated greenhouse. Used to relieve migraines but side effects can be unpleasant.

Taraxacum officinale
Dandelion

Hardy perennial. Height in flower about 25 cm (10 in). Long, deeply toothed leaves grow from basal rosette; flowers are deep yellow. Sow seed in spring in pots or straight into soil. Root cuttings can also be taken. Leaves are added to salads; before use, cover plants for a few weeks so they are blanched and less bitter.

Thymus species
Thyme

Numerous species, some upright, others creeping. Creeping thymes reach about 2.5 cm (1 in) with a spread of 20 cm (8 in) or more. Shrubby thymes reach 30 cm (12 in) with a spread of 20 cm (8 in). Creeping thymes are useful as ground cover or for scented lawns in full sun. Seed of species can be sown on top of a gritty compost. Cultivars are increased only by cuttings; creeping thymes can be increased by division. Deadhead after flowering. The plant is safely eaten in a many dishes, but the oil should be used only on medical advice. Avoid during pregnancy.

Tropaeoleum majus
Nasturtium

Half-hardy annual. Many cultivated forms that creep or are bushy, so height and spread can vary. Height is usually 20–30 cm (8–12 in), and spread can be a metre (40 in) or more. *T. m.* 'Alaska' has variegated leaves and yellow, orange or red flowers. Good plant for a sunny garden and well-drained poor soil. If too well fed, flower production suffers. Sow early in containers, or *in situ* when danger of frost is past. Deadhead regularly. Use flowers in salads before they go over. Seeds, flowers and leaves are all edible, but treat with caution.

Urtica dioica
Nettle

Hardy perennial. Grows to 1.5 m (5 ft); in good soil the flowering tops can be even taller. Leaves are arrow-shaped and deeply serrated, with bristles that break off when touched. Grows in any soil in sun or shade. Roots can also be divided and replanted. A good butterfly plant. Used medicinally, in cooking, in organic gardening and as a dye plant.

Verbena officinalis
Vervain

Hardy perennial growing to 60–90 cm (24–36 in) when in flower. Leaves are deeply lobed; flowers pale lilac. Sow seed in spring in pots or straight into soil. Grows in any well-drained soil in full sun. Divide existing plants in spring or autumn. Avoid during pregnancy.

Viola officinalis
Violet

Hardy perennial that can reach 20 cm (8 in), depending on species. Leaves, usually heart-shaped, grow from basal rosette. Scented flowers in a range of colours; dog violet and wood violet have blue or lilac flowers. Sow seed as soon as ripe in autumn and overwinter in a cold frame. Divide or take cuttings from cultivars or a good plant of a species in spring. Grows in moderately heavy fertile soil. Flowers can be used in herbal sachets and perfumes.

Viola tricolor
Heartsease

Hardy perennial that is often grown as an annual. Grows to 30 cm (12 in). Scalloped mid-green leaves; tricoloured 'little face' flowers. Sow seed in spring in cold frame. Grows in most soils in sun or part shade. Culinary and medicinal herb.

Zingiber officinale
Ginger

Perennial tropical herb. Grown in a container from a division of its rhizome. Needs peat and loam mixture with added grit and sharp sand. Water freely in hot summer months; reduce watering towards winter. Widely used in eastern cuisines.

suppliers

HERB FARMS, NURSERIES AND SEED SUPPLIERS

Arne Herbs
Limeburn Nurseries
Chew Magna, Bristol BS40 8QW
01275 333399

Barwinnock Herbs
Barrhill, Ayrshire KA26 0RB
01465 821338

Blackbrook Herb Gardens
Blackbrook Cottage
Alderley Road
Wilmslow, Cheshire SK9 1PZ
01625 539166

Bodmin Plant & Herb Nursery
Laveddon Mill
Bodmin, Cornwall PL30 5JU
01208 72837

The Botanic Nursey
Bath Road, Arworth
Nr Melksham, Wilts SN12 8NU
01225 706597

Botanicus
The Nurseries, Ringland Lane
Old Costessey, Norwich NR8 5BG
01603 742063

Brin Herb Nursery
Flichity Farr, Inverness IV2 6XD
01808 521288

Bruisyard Vineyard & Herb Centre
Church Road
Bruisyard, Saxmundham
Suffolk IP17 2EF
01728 638281

Candlesby Herbs
Cross Keys Cottage
Candlesby
Spilsby, Lincs PE23 5SF
01754 890211

Cheshire Herbs
Fourfields, Forest Road
Little Budworth
Nr Tarporley, Cheshire CW6 9ES
01829 760578

Chiltern Seeds
Bortree Stile
Ulverston, Cumbria LA12 7PB
01229 581137

The Cottage Herbery
Mill House, Boraston
Nr Tenbury Wells
Worcs WR15 8LZ
01584 781575

Downderry Nursery
Pillar Box Lane, Hadlow
Nr Tonbridge, Kent TN1 9SW
01732 810081

Edulis
1 Flowers Place,
Ashampstead, Berks RG8 8SG
01635 578113

Elsworth Herbs
Avenue Farm Cottage
31 Smith Street
Elsworth, Cambs CB3 8HY
01954 267414

Garth Cottage Nursery
Garth Cottage, Newby Wiske
Northallerton DL7 9ET
01609 777233

Green Garden Herbs & Plants
73 Alma Road, Leeds LS6 2AH
0113 274 7940

Hardstoft Herb Garden
Hall View Cottage
Hardstoft
Pilsley, Derbys
01246 854268

The Herb Farm
Peppard Road, Sonning Common
Reading RG4 9NJ
0118 9724220

The Herb Garden & Historical Plant Nursery
Pentre Berw, Gaerwen
Anglesey LL60 6LF

The Herb Nursery
Thistleton
Oakham, Rutland LE15 7RE
01572 767658

Herbs at Myddfai
Beiliglas, Myddfai
Nr Llandovery
Carmarthenshire SA20 0QB
01550 720494

Hewthorn Herbs & Wild Flowers
82 Julian Road
West Bridgford, Notts NG2 5AN
0115 981 2861

Hexham Herbs
Chesters Walled Garden
Chollerford, Hexham
Northumberland NE46 4BQ
01434 681483

Highdown Nursery
New Hall Lane
Small Dole, Henfield
West Sussex BN5 9YH
01273 492976

Iden Croft Herbs
Frittenden Road
Staplehurst, Kent TN12 0DH
01580 891432

Jekka's Herb Farm
Rose Cottage, Shellards Lane
Alveston, Bristol BS35 3SY
01454 418878

Julia's Garden
Bryn Tirion, Pen-y-felin
Nannerch, Flintshire CH7 5RW
01352 741498

Laurel Farm Herbs
Main Road, Kelsale
Saxmundham, Suffolk IP13 2RG
01728 668223

Lisdoonan Herbs
98 Belfast Road
Saintfield, Co Down BT24 7HF
028 9081 3624

Lower Severalls Nursery
Crewkerne, Somerset TA18 7NX
01460 73234

LW Plants
23 Wroxham Way
Harpenden, Herts AL5 4PP
01582 768467

Merryweather's Herbs
Chilsham Lane, Herstmonceux
East Sussex BN27 4QH
01323 833316

Napiers Herbs
Colchester Road, Tiptree CO5 0EX
01621 815238

Norfolk Herbs
Blackberry Farm, Dillington
Nr Gressenhall, Norfolk NR19 2QD
01362 860812

Norfolk Lavender
Caley Mill, Heacham
Kings Lynn, Norfolk PE31 7JE
01485 570384

Oak Cottage Herbs
Oak House, Astley
Shrewsbury SY4 4BP
01939 210219

Old Hall Plants
The Old Hall
Barsham
Beccles, Suffolk NR34 8HB
01502 717475

The Old Mill Herbary
Helland Bridge, Bodmin
Cornwall PL30 4QR
01208 841206

The Organic Gardening Catalogue
Riverdene Business Park
Molesey Road, Hersham
Surrey KT12 4RG
01932 253666

Poyntzfield Herb Nursery
Nr Balblair, Dingwall
Ross & Cromarty IV7 8LX
01381 610352

Salley Gardens
32 Lansdowne Drive
West Bridgford, Notts NG2 7FJ
0115 9233878

Selsley Herb Farm
Waterlane, Selsley
Stroud, Glos GL5 5LW
01453 766682

Seed Sowers Training Project
Stables Christian Centre
Bolnhurst, Bedford MK44 2ES
01234 376237

Stonecrop Herbs
East Lound, Haxey
Doncaster DN9 2LR
01427 753355

Suffolk Herbs
Monks Farm
Coggeshall Road
Kelvedon, Essex CO5 9PG
01376 572456

Tavistock Herb Nursery
Hornby
Lancaster LA2 8LD
015242 22280

Trent Nurseries
Tittensor Road, Tittensor
Stoke-on-Trent ST12 9HG
01782 372395

Wye Valley Plants
The Nurtons, Tintern
Gwent NP6 7NX
01291 689253

Woodlands Cottage Nursery
Summerbridge, Harrogate HG3 4BT
01423 780765

Yorkshire Garden World
Main Road, West Haddlesey
Nr Selby YO8 8QA
01757 228279

Yorkshire Lavender
The Yorkshire Lavender Farm
Terrington, York YO60 6QB
01653 648430

SUPPLIERS OF DRIED HERBS AND HERBAL PRODUCTS

Baldwin & Co
171-173 Walworth Road
London SE17 1RW
020 7703 5550

The Cotswold Perfumery
Victoria Street
Bourton-on-the-Water
Glos GL54 2BU
01451 820698

Culpeper
Hadstock Road, Linton
Cambs CB1 6NJ
01223 891196

Findhorn Flower Essences
31 The Park, Forres
Morayshire IV36 2RD
01309 690129

Hambleden Herbs
Court Farm
Milverton, Somerset TA1 1NF
01823 401104

Neal's Yard Remedies
2 Neals Yard
London WC2H 9DP
020 7379 7662

Potters Herbal Supplies
Leyland Mills
Wigan WN1 2SB
01942 405100

Shirley Price Aromatherapy
Essentia House
Upper Bond Street
Hinckley, Leics LE10 1RS
01455 615466

The Spice Shop
1 Blenheim Crescent
London W11 2EE
020 7221 4448

Verde London
75 Northcote Road
London SW11 6PJ
020 7431 3314

SUPPLIERS OF POTS AND OTHER ITEMS SHOWN IN PHOTOGRAPHS

The Blue Door
74 Church Road, Barnes
London SW13 0DQ
020 8748 9785

Braemar Antiques
113 Northcote Road
London SW11 6PW
020 7924 5628

Cath Kidston
8 Clarendon Cross
London W11 4AP
020 7221 4000

The Dining Room Shop
62-64 White Hart Lane, Barnes
London SW13 0PZ
020 8878 1020

Fabrics Galore
52 Lavender Hill
London SW11 5RJ
020 7738 9589

Habitat
Head office: 020 7255 2545
Branches throughout the UK.

Housepoints
48 Webbs Road
London SW11 6SF
020 7978 6445

Josephine Ryan Antiques
63 Abbeville Road
London SW4 9JW
020 8675 3900

Muji
Branches in London, Manchester, Nottingham and other major cities in the UK.

Summerill and Bishop
100 Portland Road
London W11 4LQ
020 7221 4566

Tobias & the Angel
66-68 White Hart Lane
London SW13 0PZ
020 8296 0058

White & Gray
113c Northcote Road
London SW11 6PW
020 7787 8173

Woodpigeon
71 Webbs Road
London SW11 6SD
020 7223 8668

OTHER USEFUL ADDRESSES

The Herb Society
Deddington Hill Farm
Warmington
Banbury, Oxon OX17 1DF
01295 692000

National Institute of Medical Herbalists
56 Longbrook Street
Exeter, Devon EX4 6AH
01392 426022

The following carry a good selection of culinary herbs and you can order in the more unusual varieties from them.

City Herbs
New Spitalfields Market
Ruckholt Road, London E10 5PB
020 8558 9708

Hyams & Cockerton
4-14 Southville Road
London SW8 2PP
020 7622 1167

Panzer's
13-19 Circus Road
London NW8 6PB
020 7722 8596 2067

index

Picture credits and acknowledgments

Key: **a** = above, **b** = below, **l** = left, **r** = right, **c** = centre

1 & 3 l Linda Garman's home in London; **4–5 top row l & c**; **32–35** Rosemary Titterington at Iden Croft Herbs, Staplehurst, Kent; **36 a, 37 & 39** Rosemary Titterington at Iden Croft Herbs, Staplehurst, Kent; **40–41** Bruisyard Vineyard & Herb Centre, Bruisyard, Suffolk (01728 638281); **41 a** Rosemary Titterington at Iden Croft Herbs, Staplehurst, Kent; **41 b** photograph © Jonathan Buckley; **42–43** Merryweather's Herbs in Herstmonceux, East Sussex; **46** Rosemary Titterington at Iden Croft Herbs, Staplehurst, Kent; **47 & 48** Bruisyard Vineyard & Herb Centre, Bruisyard, Suffolk (01728 638281); **49** Rosemary Titterington at Iden Croft Herbs, Staplehurst, Kent; **52–53** Bruisyard Vineyard & Herb Centre, Bruisyard, Suffolk (01728 638281); **56–57** Linda Garman's home in London; **58 a** Rosanna Dickinson's home in London; **58 b & 59** Mary MacCarthy's house in Norfolk; **60–61** Rosanna Dickinson's home in London; **64 & 65 l** Linda Garman's home in London; **66–67** Linda Garman's home in London; **68** Mary MacCarthy's house in Norfolk; **70 r & 76 a** Linda Garman's home in London; **76 b, 77 & 80 l** Mary MacCarthy's house in Norfolk; **80 r** Linda Garman's home in London; **81** Mary MacCarthy's house in Norfolk; **85 & 128** Rosanna Dickinson's home in London.

Barbara Segall would like to thank Gisela Mirwis for her research and Debbie Arden, who helped to compile the list of herb farms, nurseries and seed suppliers.

Rose Hammick would like to thank Carol Hammick and Adam Tindle for the use of the glasshouse and vegetable garden, Claire Farrow and William Morris, Zosia at White and Gray, Victoria Robinson, Amanda and Sarah Vesey, Georgina Hammick, Katie Rudaz, Richard Mole, Charlotte Packer, Clementine Young and Ashley Western.

The publishers would like to thank the following organizations for providing information and photographic locations:

Bruisyard Vineyard & Herb Centre
Church Road, Bruisyard
Saxmundham, Suffolk IP17 2EF
01728 638281
The 4 hectare (10 acre) site incorporates a vineyard, a winery, a herb garden, a water garden, a children's play area and a picnic area. Producers of award-winning Bruisyard English wines and a wide selection of herbs.
Pages **40–41, 47, 48, 52–53**.

Iden Croft Herbs
Staplehurst, Kent
01580 891 432
www.herbs-uk.com
Plants, seeds and garden visits. Themed show gardens include culinary, medicinal, patio, potpourri and cottage gardens.
Pages **32–35, 36 a, 37, 39, 41 a 46, 49**.

Mary MacCarthy
01328 730 133
Decorative paintwork and murals.
Pages **58 b, 59, 68, 76 b, 77, 80 l, 81**.

Merryweather's Herbs
Merryweather's Farm, Chilsham Lane
Herstmonceux, East Sussex BN27 4QH
01323 833 316
Owners Ian & Liz O'Halloran. A unique project creating 2.2 hectares (5½ acres) of gardens and wildlife habitat and incorporating a small nursery.
Pages **42–43**.